LOVING AN ADULT CHILD
OF AN ALCOHOLIC

LOVING AN ADULT CHILD

OF AN ALCOHOLIC

DOUGLAS BEY, MD, and DEBORAH BEY, RN

M. EVANS
Lanham • New York • Boulder • Toronto • Plymouth, UK

Published by M. Evans
An imprint of The Rowman & Littlefield Publishing Group, Inc.
4501 Forbes Boulevard, Suite 200, Lanham, Maryland 20706

Estover Road, Plymouth PL6 7PY, United Kingdom

Distributed by NATIONAL BOOK NETWORK

Library of Congress Cataloging-in-Publication Data

Bey, Douglas, 1938–
    Loving an adult child of an alcoholic / Douglas Bey and Deborah Bey.—
1st ed.
        p   cm.
    Includes index.
    ISBN-13: 978-1-59077-117-4 (pbk. : alk. paper)
    ISBN-10: 1-59077-117-6 (pbk. : alk. paper)
        1. Adult children of alcoholics—Psychology.   2. Alcoholics—Family
relationships.   3. Interpersonal relations.   I. Bey, Deborah, 1951–   II. Title.
HV5132.B49 2007
362.292′4—dc22

                                                                            2006102388

∞ ™ The paper used in this publication meets the minimum requirements of
American National Standard for Information Sciences—Permanence of Paper for
Printed Library Materials, ANSI/NISO Z39.48-1992.

Manufactured in the United States of America.

*To adult children of alcoholics
and those who love them—
we hope you will be
as happy as we have been.*

CONTENTS

CONTENTS

ACKNOWLEDGMENTS

We want to thank Dr. Claudia Black, who inspired us to write this book. She was kind enough to read our manuscript, make helpful suggestions and endorse it. We have recommended her books to our patients for years and appreciate the help she has given to thousands of individuals through her lectures and writing.

We would like to thank our patients and their families who have shared with us their experiences and the stories of their relationships. The material they provided has been disguised to protect their privacy.

Thanks to our literary agent, Bert Krages, for his support and guidance through the process of writing and publishing this book. He not only did his job as an agent but also threw in a little counseling as well. When Dr. Bey complained to Bert about the length of time it took to get a book published, Bert responded, "Yes, publishing takes a long time—it is not like the *immediate results* you are used to in psychiatry."

The staff at Rowman & Littlefield deserve special thanks for their assistance in producing this book and for putting up with two old novice writers like us. Some of the Rowman & Littlefield team who were especially helpful to us include Rick Rinehart, Katherine Smith, Dulcie Wilcox, Bridgette Moore, and Gail Fay.

We want to thank Linda Tippey, LCPC, who helped both of us remember our childhood experiences and the behavioral patterns we developed to cope with them. She introduced Deborah to the concept of adult children of alcoholics, and Deborah, in turn, educated Dr. Bey.

Special thanks to "Our Lady of PATH" Karen Zangerle, for her suggestions, corrections, and input; Lisa Bower, for reviewing the document and giving us the benefit of her experience and wisdom; Garold "Bud" Cole, for his expertise and input; Jerry Parsons, for his help and advice; Sally Kinsell, for her willingness to read the book and share her insights with us; and Sally Lamb and Gene Naden, for giving us some helpful feedback to improve the book. Dr. Gabriel Telot has been our mentor, friend, and member of the family for more than forty-five years. We thank him for his support and guidance as well.

Wendy Rosendale and Vicky Scott run our psychiatric office and provide special care to our patients and their families. Gene Peterson, MA, MDiv; Dr. Karen Mark; Naomi Wilansky, LCSW; and Nancy Peterson, LCSW, are all independent practitioners working in our office providing excellent care to patients.

We want to acknowledge our wonderful grandchildren: Keslie Ward, Audrey White, Kyle Ward, Andy White, and little Rachel White. We also want to recognize our children: Cathy and Dan Ward, Barbara and Bill White, Sarah Bey, Matthew Bey, and our godson, Alvis Martin. We have not been perfect parents or grandparents, but, despite our shortcomings, our children and their children have turned out to be unique, outstanding individuals. We love you and are very proud of you.

Thanks once more to Greg, Chuck, Eddie, Mary Jo, Mike, Cindy, Trish, Winnie, Roy, Beverly, and all of the gang at Jim's Steak House, who have cheered us on and been our friends over the years.

Finally, we want to thank our patients and their significant others who read copies of the manuscript for this book and found it helpful. We hope that the book, in its final form, will be as well received and as useful to adult children and their partners outside of our practice.

INTRODUCTION

Win the Heart of an ACOA, Laissez Les Bon Temps Rouler!
—ANONYMOUS

W e have worked with adult children of alcoholics (ACOAs) and their significant others throughout our professional careers. Together, we have over seventy years of clinical experience working directly with these patients. Deborah Bey is an adult child. She read the ACOA literature and went through therapy prior to meeting and marrying Dr. Bey. She trained at Barnes Hospital in St. Louis and was the head nurse on a hospital chemical-dependency unit for a number of years. She later worked in a multidisciplinary private psychiatric group practice with Dr. Bey, where she counseled adult children on an individual and group basis.

Several members of Dr. Bey's family suffer from affective illness. He trained at the Menninger Clinic, then served in the Army for two years before starting his private, multidisciplinary practice of psychiatry. He has worked with many adult children and their partners over the years. Dr. Bey is a Distinguished Life Fellow of the American Psychiatric Association; has served as a board examiner for the American Board of Neurology and Psychiatry for many years; and was past president of his county medical society, his hospital medical staff, and his county board of health. He's published a number of scientific papers as well as *Wizard 6*, the recently released memoir of his year as division psychiatrist in Vietnam.

Throughout our years of counseling adult children, we have recommended that ACOAs, and those who are in relationships with them, read the ACOA literature to help them learn the patterns of behavior they developed to survive as children in an alcoholic home and to understand how these patterns affect their adult relationships. The book we have most frequently suggested is Claudia Black's *It Will Never Happen to Me*. However, it was frequently the spouse or non-ACOA who brought the couple in for treatment because he or she was unable to understand the adult child's seemingly irrational behavior in the relationship. Nearly 20 percent of the population of the United States has an alcoholic parent and most of these individuals are involved in some sort of a relationship. As a result, we attempted to find a book to offer to persons who were in a relationship with an adult child but were unsuccessful. We contacted Claudia Black for a recommendation, and she said that she wasn't aware of a good book devoted to this topic and suggested that we write one. This was the conception of *Loving an Adult Child of an Alcoholic*

We recommend Claudia Black's books to ACOAs because readers report that they see themselves in the examples she presents. For this reason, many disguised examples of couples' experiences are included in *Loving an Adult Child of an Alcoholic*. Hopefully, readers will see themselves and their relationships in our book. We anticipate that in many cases, our book will be purchased by an adult child who is now seeking a stable, loving, committed relationship.

It is likely that your partner gave this book to you as a guide to better understand her or him and an aid to help you both develop the deep, loving, committed relationship that both of you are seeking. It is now well-known that the patterns of behavior described by adult children of alcoholics apply to many other non–chemically dependent family situations as well. Children in families with mental illness, physical disabilities, abuse, parental death, compulsive behaviors by the parents, divorce, and very large families may develop similar patterns of behavior to survive their childhood situations. It is possible that the non–adult child reading this book will identify with some of the ACOA patterns.

Loving an Adult Child of an Alcoholic may have an even wider application in the realm of the human psyche. The basic premise of the book is that patterns of behavior that were developed during childhood carry over into adult life. Recognizing these patterns and changing the ones that cause problems in adult relationships is helpful regardless of the background of the individuals involved. Couples who explore their childhood patterns and their effect on their adult lives will enjoy a deeper relationship than many partnerships experience.

The message of *Loving an Adult Child of an Alcoholic* is positive. We have a great relationship in our marriage, and most of our ACOA patients over the years have had happy marriages. As a group, ACOAs are a wonderful group of people, and we have always enjoyed working with them in our practice. They are survivors who are usually sensitive to the feelings of others, loyal, humble, and hardworking. They are hard on themselves but nice to everyone else. Most, prior to learning about ACOA patterns, have been through some bad relationships and are eager to have and appreciate a good one.

Our approach is not the only way to help your adult child change patterns nor is it the only route to a good relationship. We know of individuals who have overcome their childhood trauma without help from anyone and who seem to be capable of having a good relationship. We have seen couples who have both had difficult childhood experiences who have helped each other without any apparent outside assistance. Our religious faith has been important to us as individuals and as a couple. We have seen others who have benefited similarly from their involvement with religion and also some who appear to be doing well without any religious affiliation. *Loving an Adult Child* is a compendium of ideas that have worked in our own relationship and that have been helpful to many of the couples we have worked with over the years. We hope that some of them will be of help to you.

All of us have patterns of behavior we developed in childhood, and we unconsciously carry them over into our adult lives and relationships. To change those that get in the way of our happiness and cause problems in our relationships we have to first want to change. Then we can attempt to figure out these behavioral patterns and their childhood roots. Armed with insight into our adult patterns of behavior we can catch ourselves after we repeat the behavior. With time we may be able to catch ourselves at the time we are doing it, and, finally, we may be able to anticipate how we would have reacted in the past and, instead, make a conscious choice to act differently. When we make ourselves behave other than the way we were accustomed to act, we are changing our identity. We may be uncomfortable with the change at first. It may be helpful to imitate persons who have traits we wish to adopt and then, in time, become comfortable with our new identity. This process applies to all of us regardless of our childhood experiences. It is a process that takes considerable time and motivation to execute. We believe that any couple can take this approach and apply it to their relationship with positive results. If both persons are willing to look at themselves and attempt to change those childhood patterns that are causing difficulties in their adult relationships, they eventually will be able to do so. Discussing the childhood roots of adult problems with one another will lead to a richer relationship.

Unfortunately, many couples who seek marriage counseling come with a "DNR" (do not resuscitate) sign on their relationship. They have already decided to break their commitment to one another and are looking for someone to confirm their marriage is hopeless. Others come because their divorce lawyer told them it would look good if they sought help. Some want to show their friends and families they tried everything before giving up on the marriage. Many second marriages fail because couples repeat the same mistakes they made in the first marriage. They continue to think their problems and the solutions to those problems are external to themselves. As a result, they don't change. Alcoholics Anonymous's definition of insanity is "continuing to do the same behavior and anticipating different results."

If your partner gave you this book, he or she is not making that mistake. Your companion has concluded that *unconsciously* she or he has been seeking partners who fit the roller-coaster, off-and-on type of relationship your companion had with her or his alcoholic parent as a child. Your partner realizes that her or his relationship problems have not been due to fate, but rather to this unconscious repetition compulsion that has recreated her or his childhood situation. As they say in Alcoholics Anonymous, "If I am not the problem, there is no solution." Your partner cares enough about you to make her or himself vulnerable by sharing past experiences and exposing the patterns of behavior she or he is repeating in adult life. Hopefully, you will honor the trust that is being placed in you and will be equally open and introspective in return. If you are, you have an opportunity to develop a wonderful relationship.

We believe that you as a couple, without knowing you personally, stand a good chance of having a better relationship than most couples enjoy. We say this because your adult child has insight into his or her self and is motivated to change. You are both committed to paying attention to your relationship and working on it. Your partner is reflecting on his or her childhood experiences and how the defensive patterns developed to survive in the alcoholic home are now affecting his or her adult behavior. Your partner chose to confide in you because you appear to be a stable, caring person who is dependable and who seems to want a lasting relationship. Your partner's introspection will cause you to think of your own childhood and how it may affect your adult reactions. You will both consider the type of relationship you want to have and then think about the steps that need to be taken to achieve it. As you discuss the roots of your adult behavior together, you will find that you are forming a more intimate relationship than most couples enjoy. The psychological tools you will be developing can be utilized to solve nearly all difficulties that arise between you in the future.

We have been there, and we can attest to the fact that understanding each other's past experiences and their influence on the present relationship has made us more tolerant of each other. Recalling our own childhood experiences, the defenses we developed to cope with these events, and determining how these patterns have affected our adult relationships have helped us change ourselves for the better. By supporting each other in our efforts to improve ourselves, we were able to create the type of partnership we both wanted. This ongoing process leads to an interesting and wonderful marriage. It is a lifelong process that continues to be intriguing. We are still discovering things about each other and our relationship deepens with time. This book is our attempt to share what we have learned about this process from our patients, the literature, and from each other. We hope that this information will facilitate your understanding of your adult child and assist the two of you in your efforts to create a wonderful relationship.

YOU AREN'T READING
THIS BY ACCIDENT

It took a huge leap of faith for your partner to expose his or her childhood patterns of behavior to you—a risk taken out of care for you and your relationship. As a child in an alcoholic family, your partner was taught to cover up the family secret and suppress all feelings. Thus, when asked as an adult how she or he is doing, your partner will likely answer "Fine," no matter what is really going on. Distrust, fear of abandonment, and sensitivity to criticism are all major issues for your adult child.

By the time you met your adult child, he or she was probably already in the process of changing childhood patterns. Adult children of alcoholics have learned that their feelings and actions are not governed by outside events but by attitudes and thoughts from childhood. From reading the ACOA literature, introspection, and possibly counseling, your partner may have determined that previous relationship difficulties were not caused by fate. Instead, an unconscious attraction to the off-and-on type of relationship experienced with an alcoholic parent had been responsible for previous unhappy choices. The key attributes that your partner has are motivation and willingness to change, a realization that his or her adult difficulties are due to internal rather than external factors, and a love for you that enables him or her to overcome that fear of being abandoned and hurt.

Robin Norwood, in her book *Women Who Love Too Much*, notes that the Greeks described two types of love. The first is *eros*, which is a passionate, obsessive, all-consuming love. The second is *agape*, which is love in a partnership of two caring people who are deeply committed. Your ACOA has decided that the excitement, drama, mystery, and yearning that go with the first type of love were, in fact, an unconscious attraction to the off-and-on relationship she or he experienced as a child with the addicted parent. The agape form of love is unknown to your partner as, prior to developing insight, this type of relationship seemed to be rigid, lifeless, and boring. Your adult child has made a conscious effort to find an individual who is capable of devotion, understanding, companionship, and mutual support. That is how you got into the picture.

WHAT BEHAVIORS DO YOU RECOGNIZE?

Briefly, here are a few of the common patterns of behavior that are associated with ACOA. You may recognize your partner's behavior in some if not all of the examples.

- ACOAs tend to underestimate their attractiveness and abilities.
- These adequate-appearing individuals have some childlike qualities that are also appealing. Because there was a dearth of adult role models available while growing up, ACOAs now act the way they think adults act while inwardly retaining childish traits. As they say in the ACOA groups, "We may not have had the happiest childhoods, but we certainly have had the longest."
- Adult children seem to be ideal companions, people who are intensely passionate, powerfully attracted to their partner, sensitive to their partner's feelings, and eager to please. However, at about the time in a relationship when a partner begins to think things are really on the right track, the adult child may suddenly blow

up and accuse his or her partner of being selfish, unfaithful, or of wanting to get out of the relationship. At this point, adult children may say they do not want to see their partner again, but then might be upset that the partner doesn't call. This pattern of behavior will be repeated in a relationship.

- When life is stressful, adult children appear calm and in control. Strangely, when things seem to be calm, adult children will likely become tense.
- Adult children have a hard time trusting their partner 100 percent.
- ACOAs sometimes misconstrue what their partner says to them.
- If their companion keeps them waiting or appears to slightly ignore them, adult children may react with anger.
- Some ACOAs wait until the last moment to do things and then act as if it is a crisis. A financial crisis may result from impulsive overspending.
- Adult children tend to tell their partner what they think that individual wants to hear rather than the true story.
- Adult children may view minor setbacks as major catastrophes.
- ACOAs assume negative outcomes, including in their relationships.
- Adult children control their feelings and do not expose their thoughts.
- Adult children feel the need to control those around them. They feel anxious when they are not in the driver's seat (for example, when flying in an airplane). Games, playful activities, and spontaneity are difficult and may be avoided.
- ACOAs seem to remain on the periphery of social events.
- ACOAs have difficulty setting boundaries. It is difficult for them to say no to demands from others and equally difficult for them to ask for help when they need it. Altruism is carried to the point of burnout.
- Adult children have a tendency to become compulsive about shopping, drinking, gambling, and other addictive behaviors.
- Insecure in the role of a parent, ACOAs hope to correct the deficiencies of their own childhood. They tend to be black-and-

white thinkers and are frequently too lenient or too rigid when dealing with their children.

- Adult children may not remember much about their childhood but will reveal that they had an alcoholic parent.

COMMON CHILDHOOD EXPERIENCES

Later you will learn from your partner that during childhood, she or he experienced psychological and possibly physical abuse. Your partner was pressured to deny the reality of the home situation and, as a result, came to doubt his or her perceptions. Your ACOA's parents gave confusing answers that contradicted his or her own observations. For example, your partner may have heard "I'm not an alcoholic" from her or his obviously intoxicated father; or "Daddy's fine," when he's passed out in a puddle of vomit on the living room floor; or "We're happy," when the parents have been fighting since the previous evening. Alice said that her inebriated father would run stop signs. She remembered saying, "Daddy—you didn't stop at that stop sign," and her father would reply, "I'll stop twice tomorrow."

Adult children may have had unrealistic expectations placed on them when they were young—by themselves as well as others—reinforcing their already low self-esteem. For example, some adult children were not permitted to play, to show emotions, or to express their thoughts. They may have been told, "You want to cry—I will give you something to cry about." To keep the peace, adult children tried unsuccessfully to control their emotions, their thoughts, and their parent's irrational behaviors. Perfectionism may have represented an early attempt to offset the parental criticism they received and, in a magical way, to stop their parent from drinking. Some children may have substituted water for vodka in the liquor bottle or let the air out of the parent's car tires to keep their parent from driving and getting into an accident. Inwardly, they may have felt like failures when these attempts didn't get a parent to stop drinking.

In addition, these children experienced contorted or reversed parent-child relationships. Instead of playing with other kids, they may have been cooking meals, cleaning the house, looking after younger siblings, or caring for their intoxicated or hungover parent. Because of the constant crises in the family, adult children felt frustrated and anxious throughout childhood. Mealtimes could be tense, with the family wondering if the alcoholic would show up and, if so, in what condition. In the same way, holidays, special occasions, and school activities were dreaded. The worst-case scenarios were anticipated and often realized.

These children also learned not to trust because they were frequently lied to and disappointed by their parents. Parental statements such as "I will be at your game Friday," "Of course we are coming to your recital," or "I will pick you up after school" were proven to be unreliable. Consequently, they learned to be fearful of the outside world and to distrust authorities and institutions as well.

As kids, adult children felt that had they been lovable and worthy, their needs might have been met. These experiences all took a toll on their self-esteem and self-confidence.

Nearly one out of five (18 percent) persons in the United States has an alcoholic parent, so there is no reason to feel like the Lone Ranger. ACOAs aren't handicapped. Sometimes the traits adult children developed to cope with childhood trauma even lead to fame and fortune in adult life (Presidents Reagan and Clinton, Winston Churchill, Chuck Norris, Rod Steiger, and Suzanne Somers, to mention a few). Of course, being famous does not mean you did not suffer. When a Nobel Prize laureate was told, "You must be very happy to receive such a prestigious award," he answered, "If I was truly happy, I would not have sought this award." Rod Steiger was asked, "If you had the choice of having the childhood you experienced with your alcoholic mother and being the famous actor you are today, or having a loving, secure childhood and not being famous, which would you take?" Mr. Steiger replied, "A loving, secure childhood in a New York minute."

The process of loving an ACOA is frequently emotionally explosive. The non-ACOA can facilitate the development of the partnership by understanding the genesis of the loved one's patterns, how these behaviors are likely to affect the relationship, and what he or she, the non-ACOA, can do to respond in a positive way. There are emotional "bombs" going off for the adult child, and just as the word *bomb* can mean either a scary, explosive, device or something great, these emotional bombs characterize the nature of your relationship—scary and great.

We have been through the process ourselves. Dr. Bey has worked with many adult children and their significant others in his private psychiatric practice over the past thirty-five years. Deborah Bey, RN, is an ACOA who went through a program of recovery and later worked as the head nurse on a chemical-dependency unit, and for the past fourteen years, Deborah has been Dr. Bey's office nurse. We have a deep relationship and a happy marriage, one that has lasted seventeen years and counting. Deborah has counseled many adult children and their partners, and we both have seen the difficulties the non-ACOAs have had understanding the behavioral patterns their loved ones exhibit and the stress that this misunderstanding has on their relationships. We have attempted to instruct the non-ACOAs about the ACOA patterns and provide advice as to how they should best respond help reduce difficulties in their relationships.

SIMILARITIES AND DIFFERENCES AMONG ADULT CHILDREN

Adult children are not all cut from the same mold, but they do have common patterns of behavior. There are generally four roles that children in alcoholic homes tend to assume.

The responsible child, or the "hero," is usually the oldest. He or she grows up assuming the responsibility the parents shirk. This child brings his or her parents home from bars, looks after the younger siblings, takes over many household chores, nurses the parents when they are ill, and misses having a childhood him or herself. This child tries to solve the family's problems, ignoring his or her own needs while seeking to make up for their parents' and their family's shortcomings. The hero sees his or her mission as bringing honor to the family or dying in the effort to do so; as the ancient Greek mothers used to tell their warrior sons, "Come back with your shield or on it." These children usually become highly successful and hardworking adults who are serious and have difficulty playing. Even when successful, they feel inadequate and guilty. The adult heroes do good works out of compulsion and frequently are the victims of burnout later in life. They are caretakers who may run themselves into the ground physically and mentally by compulsively looking after others.

The acting-out child, or the "scapegoat," gets into trouble, taking the family's focus off the addicted parent and the problems within the family. This child is aware of her or his anger and expresses it directly in rebellious, antiauthoritarian behavior. The scapegoat is at risk for accidental injury and difficulties with the law. As adults these individuals are in touch with their feelings but frequently have problems adjusting to society. They tend to be self-destructive, are sometimes abusive to others, and are at risk for chemical dependency.

The adjuster, or "lost child," goes along with the program and withdraws to his or her room. This child is quiet and is often overlooked by teachers and by the family. As adults the adjusters do not feel they have any control over their lives. They tend to be shy, withdrawn, and passive in relationships. They feel lonely but tend to remain isolated, sometimes turning to material things, food, or even alcohol to try to offset their emotional void.

The placater, or "mascot," tries to please everyone else and keep them happy. This child is hyperactive, always the center of attention. Unfortunately, in some instances this behavior results in the prescription of Ritalin, which does nothing for overactive behavior that is based on a family role rather than a physiologic abnormality. Treatment by drugs may predispose the child to chemical dependency in later life. As adults placaters are sensitive to the feelings of others, assuming the caregiver role, though they are sometimes too tolerant of other people's behavior and end up in masochistic relationships. Sometimes they are the center of attention through invalidism and preoccupation with physical complaints. Their clowning and performance keep their true thoughts and feelings hidden, and they maintain an emotional distance from others. Mascots divert the family's attention from the real problem.

Individual children may take on a blend of these four roles.

A PERSON CAN HAVE MORE THAN ONE PROBLEM

This would seem to be an innately obvious statement, and yet people seem to forget it in their effort to lump all difficulties under one label.

For example, a depressed patient goes to an internist who discovers the patient is hypothyroid (or anemic, or has mitral valve prolapse [MVP] or sleep apnea). "Well, there's your problem—no wonder you were depressed," the doctor says as he puts the patient on thyroid medicine (or iron or a beta-blocker, or gives them a CPAP [continuous positive airway pressure] machine). In most cases, the patient has depression *and* hypothyroidism, MVP, or sleep apnea. In the same way, your companion's discovery that she or he has the patterns associated with being an adult child of an alcoholic does not mean your partner cannot have other disorders as well. Addictions, major psychiatric illnesses, and personality disorders may be present.

SELF-DIAGNOSIS MAY NOT BE ACCURATE

A surprising number of individuals pick their own labels. Years ago we had a patient who had several admissions for a paranoid psychosis. On the psychiatric unit he was distant, suspicious, and did not relate to other patients or the staff. He was ashamed of being labeled a "psychiatric patient." On his fourth admission he decided that the two to three beers he had most evenings qualified him to be an alcoholic. His doctor went along with his self-diagnosis and transferred him to the chemical-dependency unit. The patient loved it. He became an active member of Alcoholics Anonymous and proudly told others that he was an alcoholic.

A professional we once knew told other staff members and patients that he was an adult child of an alcoholic. It soon became apparent that this was the least of his problems. He had a grandiose sense of entitlement, he was addicted to medication and gambling, embezzled funds from his employer, was a pathological liar, and was unable to maintain appropriate boundaries with patients. He may have been an adult child, but those patterns had little to do with his sociopathic and narcissistic propensities.

If your partner is making a real effort to understand and change ACOA patterns and you are doing your best to follow the suggestions in this book and find that you are running into difficulty, consider the possibility that there are other problems present that have not been recognized and addressed. For example, if the character (Alex Forrest) played by Glenn Close in the 1987 film *Fatal Attraction* happened to have an alcoholic parent, it is unlikely that the information in this book would have helped her relationship problems or prevented her from becoming a rabbit-boiler. Some individuals unconsciously identify with their addicted parents and may themselves become self-centered, manipulative, or abusive as a result. These are not typical patterns of adult children, but, if present, they are behavior problems that need to be addressed and changed if the individuals are to become capable of enjoying healthy adult relationships.

YOUR CHILDHOOD EXPERIENCES

Learning your companion's childhood patterns will cause you to think of your own. If you share your background with your companion, he or she will help you become aware of sensitive areas and behaviors in your adult life caused by your childhood experiences. It is possible that your adult behavioral patterns fit one of the four ACOA roles described earlier. Knowing yourself and sharing your insights with your partner is one of the greatest contributions you can make to the relationship. In order to be intimate you must first know yourself intimately. Your ACOA could help you recognize and change your own childhood patterns that may be causing difficulties for you in your adult life.

The benefits of sharing your childhood experiences cannot be overemphasized. Such sharing results in increased intimacy and trust in your relationship. It helps you in your efforts to gain greater insight into your own adult behavior. It leads to a deeper mutual analysis of problems in the relationship as they arise. And, probably most importantly, it helps your ACOA partner to realize that they are not alone in having had a dysfunctional childhood. Your partner will tend to see you as the healthy member of the relationship. This is flattering, but do not accept this role. In our experience, couples who are attracted to one another usually have the same degree of problems to work out. There is a risk that your adult child will want to see you as their savior in the relationship. It is good for both of you to have a higher power to turn to, but make sure that your partner does not think you are it.

Jack was a college English professor whose father and grandfather had also been professors. Because of his background and training, Jack dressed and spoke like an academic. His second wife, Marion, was an aerobics instructor who grew up in a blue-collar family with an alcoholic father. Jack said that, initially in their relationship, Marion tended to defer to him. He quickly pointed out to her that there are many kinds of intelligence in the world and that she was a survivor who had many talents that he lacked, including several that were yet unrealized. Jack said, "Your greatest fear is that of rejection, and you experienced this when you were most vulnerable as a child. You survived that experience." Jack told Marion, "Remember the Kansas State Motto 'Ad astra per aspera,'—to the stars through adversity—which is how your life has gone; you are a star." With such comments, Professor Jack boosted his partner's self-esteem and self-confidence.

In addition to pointing out your partner's strengths, the best thing you can do for your ACOA is to share your own past and ask for help figuring out the sources of your adult behavioral patterns. By making yourself vulnerable to your partner, you are demonstrating your trust in him or her, which, in turn, enables your ACOA to feel more trusting of you. By exposing your childhood experiences, you are giving the message that you are equal partners in the relationship, that you are not the healthy one doing all the helping. You are both learning about one another and helping each other gain insight and become stronger individuals. You accept criticism from your partner because you know he or she loves you and has your best interest at heart. Through this process, the two of you will be talking at a deeper level than most couples are able to communicate. This leads to a more intimate and more interesting relationship.

When we asked our female ACOAs to pick a favorite fairy tale, most said *Cinderella*. If you are male and your adult child is female, you do not want to be her Prince Charming, as seductive as this identity might be to you. As Professor Jack realized, a fifty-fifty relationship is the goal. You want to help your companion build her or his self-confidence and self-esteem in becoming all she or he can be in life. You cannot replace the things your partner missed as a child, and you do not want to try to do this. Help your adult child in the effort to change, but do not attempt to do it for her or him. Should your partner depend on you as an idealized parental figure, she or he will soon become angry with you when she or he eventually feels controlled by dependency on you—even if you are the nicest person in the world. It will be very helpful to your partner if you express your desire to hear all aspects of her or his past experiences—the good, the bad, and the ugly—and that you love your adult child "as is," that is, unconditionally. Empathize with your companion and validate her or his feelings. As Jack pointed out to Marion, adult children are survivors. They have learned to survive multiple crises as children, and they get through difficulties in adult life as well. Codependent individuals confuse pity with love and try to heal wounded individuals. You do not want to assume this role in your relationship. Do not, however, underestimate the power of love. John Bradshaw dedicates his book *Healing the Shame That Binds You*, "To Nancy, my wonderful wife, who heals my toxic shame by loving me unconditionally."

YOUR PARTNER WILL HELP YOU

One middle-aged, professional non-ACOA named Bill said that his mother had left the family when he was a child, and as a result, he had always been jealous and controlling in relationships. He was at the early dating stage of his relationship with Vicky, a young adult child who was also dating other men. Bill asked Vicky how dating him affected her relationship with the other guys. She said, "I try to remember to yell out the right name when I have an orgasm." Bill was shocked but later said it was the "kick in the butt" he needed to drop his paranoia about rejection and his controlling behavior.

Later in their relationship, Bill and Vicky were out together at a restaurant and were approached by a man who was obviously trying to put the moves on Vicky. He told Bill how fortunate he was to have found such a beautiful young woman (Bill was ten years older than Vicky). Vicky was ignoring the compliments, so the man turned to her and said, "I will bet you were attracted to Bill because he is such a smart, successful person." Vicky looked up and said, "No, it was the sex." The man was shocked and excused himself. Bill said he laughed out loud and it won his heart.

Vicky experienced a series of roller-coaster relationships prior to meeting Bill. She said that she finally figured out that her poor relationships were not due to fate but because she was drawn to men who were self-centered, addicted, and unlikely to remain committed to a relationship. "It was like I had radar for jerks," she said. "I could go into a room and if there were ninety-nine good guys and one jerk—I would, unconsciously go directly to him." It finally dawned on Vicky that most of her problems were internal rather than external. She made a conscious effort to date Bill, who was a steady, stable person who wanted and seemed capable of having a close, trusting, committed relationship. Revealing her childhood patterns to Bill made Vicky feel vulnerable and frightened, but she wanted this relationship to work and felt Bill was "worth the risk."

George dated Alice for the same reason. He had previously been involved with unstable, addicted women and had finally concluded that it would be easier not to date at all. If there was a dating service where you could have a relationship for about an hour and a half he might sign up, but he did not think he could handle anything longer than that. Loneliness finally caused George to try to figure out why he couldn't have a lasting relationship. Having read some of the ACOA literature, George concluded that he was repeating the patterns of behavior he had developed to survive as a child in an alcoholic home. He met Alice, who was different from the women he had dated in the past. "For one thing," George said, "what Alice said and thought on one day remained consistent the next. This was unique in my experience." He shared the personal insights he had acquired with Alice and explained the influence of his childhood experiences on his adult behavior.

SIMILAR PATTERNS IN NONALCOHOLIC HOMES

Behavior similar to the ACOA patterns we've discussed is seen in adults from nonalcoholic homes. Adults whose parents suffer from mental illness, have severe physical handicaps, and other dysfunctions may identify with some of these patterns. Abuse of all types, parental death, compulsive behaviors by the parents, divorce, very large families, and other problems can result in family dysfunction and cause the children to develop similar patterns of behavior. Do not be surprised if some of the descriptions of ACOA patterns apply to your own adult behavior.

PSYCHOLOGICAL-MINDEDNESS IS UNRELATED TO IQ

This may be a surprising assertion to you. Many new therapists assume that a patient with a PhD or an MD will have more psychological insight and will be able to work well in therapy. Veteran counselors know that academic degrees and IQ are unrelated to a person's ability and willingness to introspect. Many developmentally disabled persons are extremely empathetic, in touch with their own feelings, and able to utilize psychotherapy to achieve greater self-understanding and personal growth. Some high-IQ individuals are incapable of empathy. For example, there is thought to be a continuum between autism, Asperger's syndrome, and people who are mathematics whizzes. Many of these brilliant individuals are extremely competent in tasks involving the left brain but challenged when it comes to right-brain activities like being able to empathize with others. Many compensate for this deficit by studying how others react to various situations and then giving the proper response based on what they have read or intellectually think is an appropriate reaction to a given situation.

Clarice was a straight-A junior college student with a major in mathematics and a minor in physics. She became engaged to Tom, a graduate psychology student, because many of her peers were planning marriages and she felt it was a time in her life when she should be making a commitment. When her fiancé transferred to another school to obtain his PhD, Clarice remained at her college and began having an affair with another male student. She also expressed a willingness to have an affair with Tom's best friend, Sam, who was still enrolled in the college. Sam called Tom to tell him what was going on and suggested he needed to visit Clarice. Tom returned and confronted Clarice. She expressed remorse for her conduct and impulsively married Tom and joined him at his graduate school. A few months later she left him and resumed her relationship with the young man she has been involved with in college.

Clarice's parents, disturbed by her behavior, enrolled her in another university. After a year, Clarice learned she was pregnant and returned to her husband. Although they were together and ended up having children, they maintained a parallel lifestyle with each being involved in her or his own professional careers. Clarice rejected the older child and focused on the youngest, and Tom responded by being closer to the oldest. They had what family therapists refer to as a "skewed family." Clarice was very frugal and practical, while Tom tended to be flamboyant and extravagant—Clarice would buy Tom practical gifts for Christmas and his birthday, while he would purchase extravagant gifts for her. Clarice had an affair with Tom's partner. She admitted that she and her husband seldom had sex, and when they did it was unsatisfactory for her; she described reading a book while "permitting" Tom to have sex with her. Periodically, she would threaten to divorce Tom, and he would attempt to appease her by giving in to her demands at the time. Later, after the children left the home, Tom became attracted to another woman, and when Clarice again asked him to leave, he agreed and moved out of the house. Clarice was shocked. She admitted she did not mind the departure of her husband but was embarrassed by the divorce. She told her friends she thought Tom was behaving irrationally and was having a midlife crisis. She read books and articles that supported her theory. She called Tom continually, waited for him outside of his office, and once drove up on his lawn. When he remarried she called on his wedding night to scream at him and threaten him. Later, when he avoided her and appeared to be happy in his new relationship, she sent him articles that "explained" that his avoidance of her was due to "projected rage" on his part.

Clarice came to therapy wanting to discuss what she felt was irrational behavior on her husband's part. She was unable to see how her affairs, her emotional distance, and her rejection of her husband throughout the marriage might be related to Tom leaving her and seeking a new relationship. She did not connect her angry behavior with his desire to avoid her. Therapy was unproductive because of Clarice's inability to empathize or assume any responsibility for her part in her relationship problems.

We give this example because in order to have a good relationship, it is important for both partners to be able to look at their own patterns of behavior and to talk about them with one another. In order to have psychological insight, each must be capable of empathy and be in touch with his or her own feelings. Academic success and high intelligence scores are not necessarily an indication of an individual's capabilities in this area. These qualities are vital in a relationship because, with effort, you can change yourself, but you cannot change your partner or anyone else. As they say in Alcoholics Anonymous, "If I'm not the problem, there is no solution."

How in-touch are we, individually, with ourselves?

BASIC DIFFERENCES IN MEN AND WOMEN'S THINKING

John Gray, author of *Men Are from Mars, Women Are from Venus*, points out some significant differences in the way the sexes think. Whether you are an adult child or not, these are important to note when you are trying to establish a good relationship. Gray points out that women want their partners to listen, empathize, be supportive and understanding—but not offer a solution. Men, however, often think their partner wants them to solve the problem, and thus they jump in to make suggestions, which irritates their partner. For example, the wife may complain about her supervisor at work, and her husband says, "Why don't you get another job?" The wife perceives this as not being supportive and not what she wants to do or hear. In the same vein, the husband comes home worried about a problem from work and wants to isolate himself ("go to his cave" in Gray's words) and solve the problem himself. His wife, thinking that he would benefit from sharing his concerns and worries, tries to draw him out, which elicits a negative response from her husband. A woman may come home and say, "I am thinking of mowing the yard." The man, assuming that she thinks the way he does, says, "Okay." This irritates the woman, who doesn't really want to mow the yard—she was making an indirect suggestion and hoping that he would offer to do it.

John M. Gottman and Nan Silver, in their book *The Seven Principles for Making Marriage Work*, note that men become physiologically stressed quicker and stay stressed longer than women, who have learned to soothe themselves. They feel that this explains why women are more likely to bring up emotionally charged issues and men tend to avoid them. Gottman and Silver also note that relationships are important in girls' play, and women are more sensitive and skilled at discussing feelings than men. We have observed these differences in our grandchildren. The girls play house, pretend they are getting married, and discuss their feelings with one another. The boys get a stick and go outside and hit something with it. Their discussions with one another are limited and are focused on trucks, army games, and passing gas. The importance of these observed differences is that in most relationships the female partner is probably more skilled in discussing feelings and recognizing the subtleties of the relationship.

There are three important points to be made here. First, men and women think differently and couples should take this into consideration in their communication with one another. We discussed this difference in our own relationship and concluded the second point is that things go better if men try to be more feminine in their mode of thinking. That is, men need to do more sharing of their concerns and feelings and also do more listening and supporting in the relationship. These are habits that can be practiced and learned, and this is particularly important if one of the partners is an adult child. The female ACOA probably grew up without anyone to listen to her or mirror her feelings. Her male partner should make a special effort to do just that. The male ACOA grew up in a similar environment and suppressed his thoughts and feelings like all of the other members of the addicted family. Having the normal male reticence plus the suppression of feelings that goes with being an ACOA, the male adult child will have an especially difficult time sharing his thoughts and feelings with his partner, but it will be even more important that he learn to do this.

The third point is that one of the strengths of any marriage is the ability of the couple to learn from one another. If the woman is better at relationships, feelings, and decorating, then it behooves the male partner to learn from her and to defer to her talent in these areas. One-upsmanship, power struggles, or scorekeeping are not helpful in good relationships. Genuine admiration, respect, and a willingness to help and be helped will make for a healthy partnership. Many men leave the toilet seat up, irritating many wives. If you are male and know that this irritates your spouse, then change your habits and put the seat down. Putting your seat belt on when you get into the car reminds you that accidents happen and that you need to be alert when driving. Putting the seat down on the toilet reminds you that you love your wife and want to make her life as pleasant and stress-free as possible. By the same token, if you are the female, learn to remove your panty hose from the sink so that you don't irritate your man. The message is that because you love and respect your partner, you will try to change your annoying habits.

HELPING YOUR PARTNER

As your relationship becomes more intimate, you will likely be surprised by your adult child's initial emotional outbursts. From the information you have acquired, you know that these explosive episodes represent fear of abandonment and an unconscious effort to reestablish the off-and-on type of relationship experienced with the addicted parent and significant others in the past. Remain calm as this will help your ACOA relax. Affirm your love to your partner, give her or him a hug, and reassure the individual that you are not going to leave. Let your companion know you are confused by the behavior, and that it is her or his problem to solve.

Your ACOA, feeling insecure, expects to be disappointed, but your honest and dependable behavior will help him or her feel safer. Most people like predictability in their lives; your ACOA is starving for it. The two of you can organize a predictable schedule as well as rituals and traditions for the holidays and celebrations. Later, as your partner feels more secure, you can introduce nice surprises and spontaneous events that are fun. This will help the individual realize that unplanned events need not be traumatic. As John Lennon once said, "Life is what happens to you while you are making other plans." Life is not predictable. Humor is a way to introduce nice surprises into your relationship, making mutual self-discovery easier and adding zest and fun to the process.

Listening to your partner is of the utmost importance. Do so without judging and without jumping in with proposed solutions. As your companion tells you about childhood experiences, try to put yourself in her or his shoes as a child and empathize with how it must have felt growing up in an alcoholic home. Tell and show your ACOA that you love her or him. There is nothing better for people's self-worth than to have someone they love know everything about them and still love them. John Gottman and Nan Silver in *The Seven Principles for Making Marriage Work* note the importance of having an "emotionally intelligent marriage" in which the couple maintains positive feelings toward each other while dampening the negative ones. Show your partner how important her or his friendship is to you, vocalizing that you would never knowingly do anything to hurt her or him. If you should inadvertently injure your partner's feelings, be quick to apologize. Tell your partner you do not expect her or him to be perfect and that you are not going to leave when she or he is not.

As we mentioned earlier, sharing your childhood experiences with your ACOA will result in greater intimacy and boost her or his self-confidence and self-esteem. Your partner may be uncomfortable in social situations because her or his family was somewhat isolated socially and didn't make small talk. Practicing conversations with your companion at home and giving positive feedback after you go out together socially will help your partner develop confidence in her or his ability to informally socialize with others. Associating with couples who have good relationships will help provide good role models for you and will provide an atmosphere in which you are surrounded by other happy couples.

Discuss child rearing with your partner and find an approach that you can agree upon. It is important to have a united front when you approach the children. Support your partner's efforts to set boundaries for him or herself. Joining an organized religion may provide guidelines for your child-raising efforts and a good atmosphere for the whole family among other families who are trying to improve themselves.

Help your companion become more assertive. Let your partner

know that it is natural that you disagree at times and that a variance of opinion does not imply a loss of love. Practice disagreeing and compromising in your relationship, encourage your partner to say no when he or she does not feel like doing something, and encourage him or her to ask for help when it's wanted or needed.

Giving thanks for your many blessings each day will help your ACOA develop a positive attitude. Some ACOAs find it beneficial to read positive affirmations each day in an effort to reprogram the negative tapes acquired as a child.

TAKING CARE OF YOUR RELATIONSHIP WILL LEAD TO A DEEP, HEALTHY COMPANIONSHIP IN THE LONG RUN

To paraphrase Sir William Osler, the father of modern medicine, to stay healthy, one should obtain a chronic illness and take care of it. The point being, if you are aware that you have a health problem and give it your full attention, you will end up being healthier and will probably enjoy a longer life. The same applies to your current relationship. Your ACOA partner is aware that your relationship is being affected by patterns of behavior that resulted from childhood experiences and has now made you aware of this fact. You and your partner are discussing these experiences and the feelings that were engendered by them. The two of you are analyzing your adult reactions and changing those that are getting in the way of your closeness. This process of continued exploration and discussion of your relationship has the potential to result in an intimacy that is deeper and more interesting than most people experience. It also provides you with a way to solve the problems that will inevitably arise in your relationship. Finally, you are acknowledging daily the importance of your relationship, and you are both working to develop the best possible bond between you.

A FEW TIPS ABOUT CHANGING YOURSELVES

You will be helping one another acquire insight and make changes in your adult behavioral patterns. There are two parts to insight. The easiest is intellectual insight, which may be gained by reading or discussing the adult patterns of behavior that have arisen from childhood defenses. The second is emotional insight, which results from reexperiencing childhood feelings in adult relationships and recognizing them as such. It is the combination of intellectual and emotional insight that will enable you both to know yourselves and to make changes.

Over the years we have seen a number of patients who seemed to have intellectual insight into their problems but showed little change in their behavior. This would be similar to reading diet books, counting calories, and staying the same weight. Alcoholics Anonymous talks about "paralysis by analysis." (Alcoholics Anonymous is a free, volunteer organization available twenty-four hours a day, seven days a week to assist individuals in their efforts to control their disease. Most professional treatment programs rely heavily on Alcoholics Anonymous as part of their treatment program. The joke in Alcoholics Anonymous is, "Rehabilitation is a $40,000 program that teaches you that there is Alcoholics Anonymous." While there is some chiding of this nature, in general, the professionals associated with treatment programs work cooperatively with the volunteer twelve-step programs in most communities.) At some point you just have to, as the Nike ads say, "Just do it!" It takes courage for you and your partner to look at yourselves honestly. It takes motivation and patience to keep working on behavioral patterns until you can each anticipate your old ways of acting and consciously make yourself behave differently. When you both reach the point where you are able to change your adult actions, it will seem strange to you because your identity is associated with your old actions. You may feel "phony" reacting in a different way. As you are attempting to adopt a new identity, it is helpful to find someone who has the type of behavior you want to have and imitate them. Eventually you will adopt the new patterns and the new identity. For example, if you say "nurse" to a student nurse in the hospital, the individual does not look up because she or he doesn't feel like a nurse yet and does not have that identity. As the person imitates the registered nurses, she or he eventually acquires the nursing identity. Then when you say "nurse," the individual looks up and responds because she or he now has a new identity as a nurse. Likewise, when you are attempting to go from a novice to an intermediate or expert in a sport, you do well, according to psychologists, to visualize an idealized image of yourself performing perfectly. In your quest to change individually and as a couple, follow these examples—imitate an ideal couple until you have become the person and the couple you want to be.

ENTERING THE "MIND FIELD"

YOUR PARTNER CAN USE YOUR HELP

*L*oving an Adult Child of an Alcoholic is a shock-and-awe experience. We will attempt to assist you through the "mind field" of emotionally sensitive areas left over from your partner's childhood experiences. As you are able to empathize with your partner's childhood experiences and understand the reasons for his or her sensitivity and seemingly irrational adult behaviors, you will also become aware of your own sensitivities and irrational behaviors and will be able to share this information with your adult child. Your companion needs your help as recovery cannot be accomplished in isolation. This person needs someone to trust who can supply the support and validation required.

SOME PEOPLE NEVER CHANGE

As we have mentioned, your companion reached a point where she or he concluded that her or his relationship problems were internal rather than external. Some adult children never reach this point and continue to repeat their childhood paradigm of an off-and-on relationship that mimics the one they had with their alcoholic parent. They become involved with addicted individuals or persons who are undependable and likely to disappoint or hurt them. They deny their own roles in the selection of these individuals. Ralph was trained as a typesetter and had a printing business. He had been married and divorced before meeting Mandy, a young schoolteacher and a single parent. Mandy mentioned that her dad was an alcoholic and that her first husband had been an abusive alcoholic. She picked Ralph because he was handsome and seemed to be a stable individual. Mandy, however, had no real insight into her adult patterns of behavior. Ralph said that the day they returned from their honeymoon, Mandy asked him to mow the yard and trim the hedges. He said that he would but he had some business he had to attend to first. Mandy flushed and said, "You do the yard work *now* or I am out of here." Ralph said he was too shocked to respond, and she stormed out of the house and left him. A couple months later she returned, gave him a big hug and a kiss, told him this was where she belonged and that their relationship seemed right to her. Five minutes later she again walked out. Ralph was confused and even more so when he overheard her telling her former abusive husband how much she loved and missed him. He asked Mandy to go with him for counseling but she refused, stating that she did not have any problems. As they say in Alcoholics Anonymous, "Denial is not a river in Egypt." They divorced. Ralph predicted that Mandy would go back to her abusive ex-husband or would continue to run from committed relationships as she did with him. Mandy did not see any reason to introspect or to change herself.

Jessica, a young ACOA, complained about her husband Steve's self-centeredness and his addiction to his work. She was finally unable to deny that he was continually unfaithful to her. As she described her spouse and her marriage for several hours, she did not have one positive statement to say about either. However, her primary preoccupation was her fear that her abusive, selfish, unfaithful, critical, addicted husband might leave her. Intellectually, she knew that her adult situation was a repetition of the relationship she had with her alcoholic father. Emotionally, she felt powerless to change herself or to leave the marriage.

Steve thought that Jessica was "a stupid, screwed-up bitch" and that he had no psychological problems that warranted attention or change. Jessica had sound intellectual insight but emotionally was overwhelmed by her fears of abandonment. Steve thought the problems in their relationship were due to Jessica.

Kim was a partner in her husband Jerry's business. She was also an ACOA. She had been disappointed by her partners in her previous relationships and was extremely jealous of Jerry. Jerry said that when a woman customer came into the store, Kim would watch his response to the lady and then would cross-examine him later. "You saw that she didn't have a wedding ring, didn't you?" Jerry said he hadn't noticed. "I'll bet," Kim snorted. "I saw you trying to look down her dress." Jerry denied this. "She seemed to know you—did you know her before she came into the store?" Jerry said these questions would continue, and no matter what he said, Kim did not believe him and was convinced that he was having an affair with the other woman or wanted to have an affair with her. Jerry said that eventually he did have an affair. "We had no sexual relationship and I was constantly being accused. I felt I might as well go ahead and do something—I was going to be blamed whether I did or not." Eventually, they were divorced. Kim had created a self-fulfilling prophecy in which she anticipated her partner's infidelity and kept hounding him until he did just what she "knew" he was going to do. She moved on to repeat this pattern in her next relationship as well.

Jolene grew up in a home with an abusive alcoholic father and a mentally ill mother who was emotionally unavailable. After a series of abusive relationships, she married Craig, who was an abusive workaholic. "I married both of my parents," she later exclaimed. "He is both abusive and unavailable emotionally." Although Jolene seemed to understand her current difficulties, her fear of abandonment prevented her from making a change. She continued to feel trapped in what she identified as the unhappy relationship she had as a child. She was miserable but found the idea of change too frightening to seriously contemplate. She prayed constantly that God would cause Craig to stay with her. Eventually Craig left her for another woman.

Elaine was a professional who had been married twice to abusive alcoholics. She said that she was currently in love with Matthew, who was a married alcoholic. When Elaine's therapist asked her what she thought about her current situation, Elaine answered that she thought she needed to lose some weight so she would be more attractive to Matthew and then perhaps he would leave his wife for her and give up drinking. Her therapist asked how much Matthew weighed. "About 200 pounds," Elaine answered. "Then you need to lose 200 pounds," responded the therapist. Elaine said, "But he is so special and so much fun." When the therapist asked for an example of Matthew's unique qualities, Elaine said, "He showed up at my door the other night unexpectedly. He was half drunk and completely naked. He had a bottle in one hand and two tomatoes in the other." The therapist pointed out that "as attractive as that image might be, a married alcoholic who appears unannounced and nude at your door is not the most promising candidate for a long-term, healthy relationship." Elaine said intellectually she had to agree and added that a colleague had recently brought a nice-looking widower to her home. She said that this gentleman was apparently a stable individual who was about her age but she said she had absolutely no interest in the man. Some adult children give up on relationships altogether and decide that it is less painful to accept a single life. It is unlikely that these individuals would be attracted to this book on relationships.

Your partner is different from the examples above. Your ACOA opted to change him or herself, choosing you because he or she believed you would be different from past partners. You seemed to be caring and capable of a committed relationship. This was a new experience for your adult child, who took a "leap of faith" by revealing his or her adult patterns of behavior to you.

THE LEAP OF FAITH—SCARY BUT ESSENTIAL

This courageous gesture on your companion's part reminds us of a ski lesson Doug once had in Colorado. The instructor had him go to the top of an expert run that was covered with huge boulders. Doug started down the hill full of fear, crouching down on his skis (known as the security crouch among instructors). The instructor yelled from below,

"Stand up and lean out." "Lean out?" Doug thought. "You have got to be nuts." Then he thought, "I am paying this guy for this lesson, so I should try to do what he says." So, sure that he was going to do a head plant into the nearest rock, Doug leaned out and went effortlessly down the hill. Intellectually, he realized that by leaning out he was shoving his ski edges into the snow, giving him more stability, but emotionally it seemed contrary to everything his brain was telling him. Taking a chance by leaving oneself vulnerable in a relationship is like that. It is the unknown and you risk being hurt, but it is the only way to acquire a loving relationship.

Your partner took the risk of revealing him or herself to you so that you could understand your companion and so that the two of you would be able to form a good relationship. Your ACOA cares about you and wants the partnership to work. You may wonder how you got yourself into this "mind field." You did not just walk into this explosive relationship—you ran into it! You were probably head over heels in love with this sensitive, passionate individual. She or he is humble and does not seem to realize how talented she or he is. Although your ACOA may seem mature and in control on the surface, you sense an appealing childlike quality that makes you feel powerful and needed. Mitch described his initial meeting with Trudy this way: "I knew there was something unique about her early in our relationship. At times she seemed like an assertive woman, while at other times I sensed she was like a frightened little girl." Mitch said that as their relationship progressed, he saw more clearly that Trudy was both a strong survivor and sometimes a scared, needy child. Mitch said he found both aspects attractive and the combination irresistible. At times he felt he could lean on her, while at other times he felt he was the strong one on whom she depended. "It was a double whammy," he said.

THE SHOCK OF THE SHOCK-AND-AWE RELATIONSHIP

You cannot believe that this wonderful person appears to be just as in love as you are. Everything seems perfect . . . until you are hit with the first emotional explosion. The seemingly perfect person you have fallen in love with suddenly changes, and you are confronted by a person you do not know. This angry, cold individual tells you that you are selfish or accuses you of being unfaithful or screams, "I never want to see you again!" and you feel like you have been punched in the stomach. You have just experienced the "shock" of the relationship. Below are four couples who experienced this type of emotional explosion in their relationships.

Four Examples of the Shock

Lisa and Ted were at a French restaurant for a romantic candlelit dinner. They had been dating a few weeks and the relationship seemed to be progressing rapidly in a positive direction. Ted felt himself falling in love with this unique young woman. In the middle of the dinner, Lisa suddenly said, "I know what you are thinking and it is not good." "What?" asked Ted. "You know what you were thinking," Lisa retorted in a loud angry voice. "How can you tell what I am thinking?" asked Ted. "By your nonverbal behavior," screamed Lisa, who jumped up and angrily left the table and exited the restaurant before the meal was finished. Ted followed her out of the restaurant, and Lisa irately told him that she was not riding home with him, so "call me a cab." Ted kept his cool and said, "Okay, you are a cab." Lisa started laughing, and they were able to return to their table and finish dinner.

Mary was a redheaded Irish girl who had an identical twin sister, Kathleen. They grew up in an alcoholic home. Mary had been previously married to an abusive alcoholic, but she divorced him and married a quiet clinical psychologist named Bob. They celebrated Bob's birthday a few months after they were married. Mary gave him a number of gifts, including a subscription to *Playboy* magazine. When Bob sat down and opened the magazine to the centerfold, Mary stood behind him and screamed, "That is what you want, isn't it? A woman with big breasts." Mary then put her fist through the door. It was not until the next day that she settled down and was able to talk. In the meantime Bob talked to Mary's brother-in-law, who said that he'd been through similar situations with Kathleen. Bob said his discussions with his brother-in-law helped him understand his wife's shocking blowups and made it easier for him to discuss his confusion with Mary.

Elizabeth and John said they were having a nice day together when John asked, "Do you want to go to Pizza Hut?" Elizabeth erupted, "You think I have a big butt?" John was shocked and confused. "I said 'Pizza Hut,'" he responded. "Oh sure, I heard what you said," Elizabeth shouted angrily. Later, they were able to calmly discuss this interchange. Elizabeth admitted that she anticipated criticism and sometimes misperceived what others said to her. She said that she felt self-conscious and if people were laughing or looking at her in social situations, she often felt they were talking critically about her.

Kendra and Adam had been happily dating a short while. They were driving through town having a nice conversation when Adam suddenly became enraged and screamed, "Why are you looking at that guy?" Kendra was shocked and baffled. "I was not looking at anyone," she responded. Adam said he knew that she was looking at the guy on the street, and he had the feeling that she knew the fellow. Later, as they talked about this incident, Adam said that he had low self-esteem and couldn't imagine how Kendra would be attracted to him. He had the feeling that it was only a matter of time before she rejected him for someone else.

Understanding Shocks

In order to understand the emotional outbursts that surprise you, you need to recognize that both you and your partner have sensitive areas that stem from your childhood experiences. Your adult relationship is affected by these areas of hypersensitivity. We are focusing on the sensitive areas that your partner probably has, but you will likely discover your own touchy spots as well.

For example, Sarah was a college professor who did not marry until she was in her midthirties. She married Mike, who was a slightly older member of the faculty. They had discussed their childhood experiences prior to their marriage. Sarah revealed that her younger brother had committed suicide during his teenage years and that she felt considerable guilt for not being able to prevent his death. Mike shared that his father was an alcoholic and that his drinking had traumatized his family. Mike was familiar with the patterns of behavior associated with being an ACOA and shared them with Sarah. They were able to talk about their childhood experiences and adult patterns and to work out problems that came up in their relationship. After a few years of marriage, Mike began drinking to excess and showed signs of alcohol addiction. He was unwilling to consider treatment and was critical of anyone who confronted him with his illness. One evening he announced that he was going out to have "a drink with the boys." He was furious when Sarah voiced her disapproval. "You have always been possessive and jealous," he shouted. "I could be going out to have a glass of iced tea and you still wouldn't like it." Mike returned after an hour or so and said nothing to Sarah.

The next day, Sarah said, "It is apparent that you are angry with me—what is the problem?" "I told you last night," Mike answered. "You would be angry if I had a glass of iced tea; you have always been jealous, possessive, and controlling." Sarah answered, "Perhaps I have been, but I have not said anything to you until now. In case you haven't figured it out, you are an alcoholic." Mike smiled. Sarah responded, "You smile, which makes me wonder if you have accepted the problem, because if you did, you would know it is not anything to smile about. You have reacted defensively when anyone has commented on your drinking." Sarah went on to enumerate in detail her observations to support her statement that Mike was an alcoholic. She then said, "If I hear that you are telling people that I am controlling you by objecting to your going out, I will tell them why I worry when you are gone." Mike responded, "I haven't said anything about you—why are you so worried about my blaming you?" "I've thought about that," Sarah answered. "When my brother died it was a terrible trauma to us all, and we felt terribly guilty and somehow responsible for his death. Had he died from cancer or any other disease we would have received sympathy and support from others. Instead we got questions and people looking at us as though we must have caused him to take his own life. I accepted the guilt and blame for his death for years—even though I had nothing to do with his suicide. I am not going to accept the blame for your addiction nor for my worrying about your going out with the boys." Mike stayed home and attempted to control his drinking, but found that he was unable to do so and that the only solution was to go into rehabilitation and stop completely. He is actively involved in AA (Alcoholics Anonymous), and Sarah attends Alanon.

Mike and Sarah's situation illustrates again that childhood trauma produces sensitive areas for adult survivors. In this couple's relationship, Mike hated his father's drinking and was sensitive and defensive when confronted with his own addiction. Sarah felt blamed for her brother's suicide and was not going to accept the responsibility for her husband's self-destructive behavior. She also drew her boundary line when it came to worrying about him all night while he went out with his friends. In other words, she identified that Mike was an alcoholic and it was his problem. She could not cure his addiction for him and he would have to take the consequences for the behavior that resulted from his drinking.

Kevin was a young loan officer in a bank. He said that his alcoholic mother constantly accused his father of being unfaithful to her. He grew up being angry with his father for hurting his mother. When he became a teenager, Kevin started following his dad and discovered that his father wasn't unfaithful—his mother had alcoholic paranoia. Then Kevin was mad at his dad for putting up with his mother's false accusations. He vowed that he would never let himself be in that situation when he was married. Subsequently, Kevin dated and married Michelle, a blond bank teller he met at work. On their honeymoon Kevin picked up the wastebasket from the motel to take it out to the Dumpster. His new wife asked, "Where are you going, honey?" Kevin lost his temper. "It's none of your damn business where I am going," he screamed. His surprised bride wondered, "Who is this crazy angry person I married?" When they returned home, they sat down and discussed what had happened on their honeymoon. They were able to determine that Kevin reacted strongly to his wife's innocent question because it brought up his feelings from childhood toward his alcoholic, paranoid mother. It was an explosive area in his "mind field." Michelle was now aware that even benign questions about Kevin's activities would bring up negative feelings associated with his mother's paranoia. At the same time, Kevin was able to see that Michelle wasn't anything like his mother and that her questions weren't derived from suspicion on her part nor were they meant to accuse him of any wrongdoing.

Kevin told Michelle that she didn't need to tiptoe around, worrying about saying the wrong thing to him. He was the one who needed to change and remind himself that Michelle was not his mother and that she wasn't checking up on him. "I have got to remember that feelings are not facts; and that I am not going to be able to change this overnight," he said. "I will probably continue to react, but we both know what is going on and hopefully I can change this in time." Kevin and Michelle continued to talk about their childhood experiences and the sensitive areas in their adult relationship that resulted from their earlier trauma. At first the process was more of an intellectual one. Each subsequent time that Kevin reacted emotionally, he was able to associate that emotion with his rational awareness that Michelle wasn't his mother and her comments were not accusatory. This is what is known as insight—a connection between intellectual and emotional awareness. At first Kevin caught himself after he erupted and later, while he was upset. In time, he was able to anticipate situations and comments that had triggered emotional reactions in the past and consciously choose a different response. Kevin said that although he was able to anticipate and change his reactions in advance, he continued to have the same gut feeling inside when Michelle said something that reminded him of his mother's irrational behavior.

This process isn't as mysterious as it might sound. The same thing occurs in sports. You consult with a professional about being able to hit the ball harder in tennis, and the pro advises you to "put your hip into it as you swing." You understand their words but do not really understand what they are saying until one day, as you are practicing, you finally do what the pro instructed and you feel the increased power as you turn your hip while striking the ball. You return to the coach, who notes that you've executed his suggestion. He then hits the ball to you with more pace, and, under pressure, you revert to your old inefficient swing. However, as you continue to practice, you finally reach a point where putting your hip into the ball is part of every swing regardless of the pressure you are under. You have now integrated the new pattern of behavior and have insight into the solution to the problem of putting pace on the ball.

Sometimes adult children seek help from a professional for their adult behavioral problems. In this situation it is the therapist or doctor who is perceived as being similar to their alcoholic parent or some of the abusive relationships they've experienced in the past. The transferring of feelings from significant persons in the past to the therapist is referred to as transference in psychotherapy.

Barbara was a middle-aged housewife and mother. She said her memories of her childhood consisted of her alcoholic father being drunk most of the time and her mother being preoccupied with her dad and his illness. Barbara felt her thoughts, feelings, and desires were ignored when she was growing up. She was frustrated by her family's refusal to answer her questions as a child. Later, in therapy, she would berate her therapist, saying that she had gone to another doctor years before who had helped her with one session, and here she was coming week after week to her current therapist and was no better. The therapist was tempted to tell Barbara to go back and see her other therapist (the therapist's feelings in response to the patient's feelings is known as countertransference), but he realized that she would see this as another rejection in her life. He quietly noted that she seemed to be angry and disappointed with him. After several months of therapy Barbara came into her session and began quizzing her doctor about sex. He asked her, "Why all the questions on this topic?" Barbara answered angrily, "I read a magazine in the waiting room that had an article on sex. Are you going to answer me or not?" The therapist attempted to answer her questions for the remainder of the hour.

The next session Barbara remained tight-lipped and refused to talk. The therapist tried numerous times to find out the reason for her silence. Finally, after forty-five minutes, Barbara said, "You do not want me to talk." The therapist expressed surprise and pointed out he'd been coaxing her to speak for forty-five minutes. "What would make you think I did not want you to talk?" he asked. "Well, you took the magazine out of the waiting room." In the subsequent discussions with her therapist, Barbara was able to recognize that she was repeating her childhood experiences in therapy. She had reproduced a situation in which her early feelings of being rejected and ignored by her parents were repeated in her relationship with her doctor. She went on to say that she did the same thing with her husband at home. She would become furious when he looked away while she was speaking to him, and she was angry when he was quiet at the end of the day. Barbara was able to explain the childhood source of her anger to her husband. He, in turn, was able to help her recognize when she overreacted to situations in which she perceived herself to be rejected or ignored as an adult.

As previously noted, the explosive anger that catches you off guard, in most cases, is not hatred but a manifestation of your companion's fear. Your ACOA thinks that he or she is unworthy and unlovable and that it is only a matter of time before you will see through the façade and reject or abandon him or her. Adult children have difficulty with intimacy, partially because their alcoholic parent frequently disappointed them by not keeping his or her promises. As your adult child feels closer to you in the relationship, he or she becomes anxious, feeling increasingly vulnerable to disappointment and pain. To be in control of the situation, your partner may also feel the need to reject you before you reject him or her. It can be a self-fulfilling prophecy in which adult children blow up and cause their partner to leave them, which is exactly what they fear is going to happen.

Early on, your ACOA was likely attracted to off-and-on relationships that mimicked their relationship with their alcoholic parent. People tend to choose the same type of unhappy relationships again and again, hoping for resolution. For example, Anna was a daughter of an alcoholic who had been physically and psychologically abused throughout her childhood. When she was twelve, her father was diagnosed with pancreatic cancer and died suddenly. Anna said the experience of his death was terribly traumatic to her. "I desperately wanted to hear him say he loved me. I wanted to ask him why he had hurt me and treated me so badly. There were so many questions that went unanswered." Anna became an oncology nurse and worked in a cancer treatment center where she devoted her life to trying to save terminally ill cancer patients. Over and over again, she repeated the tragic experience she'd gone through with her father's death, hoping to somehow resolve the ambivalent relationship she had with her father.

Sometimes shocks are more subtle. Jennifer said she did not blow up in her relationships but would become so controlling and "bitchy" that she would cause her partners to withdraw and eventually leave her. "In retrospect, I think I was testing them to see if they would leave me or confirm my suspicion that they were going to leave," she said. Jennifer described an incident where a boyfriend gave her a necklace and later gave the same necklace to his niece. She felt devastated that she was not special to him and that her gift had been a "generic present." "I would not let go of it—I kept griping to him about it until he eventually became exasperated and stopped calling me." In another instance Jennifer went to a ball game early to save seats for her boyfriend and some other friends. After the game her boyfriend left with one of his male friends, and Jennifer felt that she'd been used and abandoned by him. "Once again, I could not stop harping about how selfish he was. I kept pointing out how I had spent most of my day saving seats for him, and he went off and left me with his buddy after the game. Needless to say he was not excited about hanging around with me to hear more of my griping."

By the time your adult child met you, she or he had decided not to settle for a roller-coaster relationship. This individual selected you as a stable and dependable person who could work toward a close and loving relationship. However, this was new territory for your companion. In the back of her or his mind, your adult child anticipated that you would fail, disappoint, and leave her or him. Your partner felt unlovable, being, as John Bradshaw describes it, a victim of toxic shame: "To have shame as an identity is to believe that one's being is flawed, that one is defective as a human being." This is a sensitive area for your partner because she or he was disappointed and hurt many times as a child. As your ACOA started falling in love with you, her or his anxiety increased because she or he felt more vulnerable and realized your departure would be devastatingly painful. Your companion perceived you as an alcoholic parent or one of the abusive individuals she or he dated before meeting you. In response to these fears of abandonment, your adult child blew up and accused you of wanting someone else or only caring about yourself.

This pattern is also an effort to reestablish a "push-pull" roller-coaster type of relationship that is familiar to your partner. In that "roller coaster" of the past, the alcoholic parent would get drunk and be self-absorbed, perhaps leaving your companion on a bar stool or in the car in front of the bar while getting drunk. The next day the parent may have been remorseful and may have attempted to make up for his or her misbehavior. As an adult, your partner may have found relationships that duplicated this paradigm in which the significant other got drunk, became abusive, and then was remorseful and loving. He or she may be unconsciously attempting to establish this type of relationship with you. This pattern can have the effect of being a self-fulfilling prophecy. The adult child screams, "I never want to see you again!" while simultaneously fearing that you will indeed leave. This behavior, if not understood, could end up driving you away.

Responding to Shocks

How should you respond to your partner's seemingly angry outburst? Let us review the event. You are in a loving relationship with your adult child and everything seems to be going well. Suddenly, your companion appears to be enraged and accuses you of being selfish and not caring about them. Your ACOA tells you to get out, that she or he cannot stand you, and that your relationship isn't going anywhere. You feel like someone just punched you in the stomach; you are in shock. Anything you say seems to make your partner angrier. What should you do? Most importantly, stay calm and be flexible. Do not answer anger with anger. Martial arts masters say that the willow bends with the wind while the rigid tree is broken. Think of how the martial arts practitioner gently deflects an opponent's blow or steps aside to allow the aggressor's force to pass harmlessly by rather than meeting it head-on. Your calmness dampens your companion's rage. Your partner is used to being with people who respond in anger and later kiss and make up. Let your partner know that you are not the alcoholic parent nor are you like the relationships she or he has had in the past. Calmly point out that you are confused by this reaction since things seemed to be going well in your relationship; you were moving to another level of intimacy when suddenly your partner blew up and falsely accused you of not caring about her or him and of wanting out of the relationship. Give your companion a hug, stating that you love her or him and aren't going to leave, but that the anger being expressed is her or his problem, not yours.

As you learn about and empathize with your partner's early experiences, you will have a better understanding of his or her seemingly irrational adult reactions. You will also start thinking of your own patterns of behavior. June was the adult child of an alcoholic father. She told her husband, Ted, that her father would take her to taverns as a child and abandon her on a bar stool to drink a Pepsi while he got drunk with his friends. She sat all day drinking Pepsi and watching her dad drink himself into oblivion. She felt bored, angry, and worried about his well-being. Ted's mother had bouts of severe depression that caused her to be bedridden for weeks at a time. He said that as June and he discussed his past, he realized that his feelings as a child were similar to hers. He recalled how he would sit in a chair in the quiet, darkened living room, chewing a hole in the knee of his pants while feeling bored, irritated, and concerned about his mother, who was upstairs in bed. As a result, both Ted and June were sensitive to being ignored or having to wait in their adult relationships. This awareness helped them understand and be able to discuss their flare-ups of irritation when situations arose that reminded them of those childhood feelings.

SIX ACTIONS YOU CAN TAKE TO HELP YOUR PARTNER AND GET THROUGH THE "MIND FIELD"

Slow Things Down

Your relationship probably started up with an intensity that was new to you. A common belief among ACOAs is that there is one special person who is their intended partner in life. If they can find this person, adult children believe, they will fall deeply in love and as a couple remain true to one another for the rest of their lives. This is a description of a codependent, addictive relationship. This is the type of interaction in which each partner tries to be what she or he thinks the other person wants rather than revealing her or his true thoughts and feelings. If you begin the relationship on this basis, you will both fall in love with the idealized façades you present to one another and will not really know each other's true selves. There is a joke in AA that goes like this: How can you tell when two alcoholics are on their second date? There is a moving van parked in one of their driveways. The point is that dependent, impulsive individuals will jump into a relationship too quickly and too intensely. Therefore, put the brakes on the relationship if you feel it is moving too rapidly and try to share who you really are—not who you think your partner wants you to be. Lust adds to the intensity of the experience. While this is exciting, it will not last. Keep in mind that forming a good relationship is a slow process. Your partner may become frightened if you want to slow down the tempo of the initial relationship, fearing that you are going to abandon her or him. You can reassure your companion that you are in this for the long haul and that really good, lasting relationships take time as you share love, sadness, anger, and joy with one another. There will be conflicts that will frighten your partner; she or he may misperceive a lack of agreement as a lack of love and may think that one must be happy all of the time in order to be lovable. Talk about your disagreements and reach compromises. This process will help to nurture your budding relationship. As your adult child verbalizes fears, she or he will feel more in control. Understanding and validating feelings will help lessen your companion's discomfort.

Be an Active Listener

An important part of love is listening. The more comfortable you are with yourself, the better listener you will be to your companion since your own frustrations and needs can get in the way of your being able to quietly listen to what your partner has to say. Someone said that we are as sick as our secrets. By listening to your partner, you can help him or her divulge those secrets and be healed, while enhancing your relationship together as well.

While trying to become an active listener, you may find yourself at a loss for words to say to encourage your partner to speak. If you do not know what to say, you can always say, "You are not telling me everything"—and you will always be right. Body language and tone of voice are as important as the actual words expressed. Do not just listen for the lyrics but hear the underlying music as well. Some therapists refer to this process as "listening with the third ear." You are listening for not only what is said but also what is not said. If you do not understand what your partner is saying, keep listening. Your partner will eventually explain it to you. It is likely that no one listened to your companion when she or he was growing up. By listening actively you are helping your adult child's self-esteem and providing her or him with an experience that is unique in her or his development. Do not give advice, do not correct them, and don't criticize. As they say in Alanon, "Say what you mean, mean what you say, but do not say it mean." Paraphrase what your companion says and reflect it back to her or him. Validate your partner's feelings whenever you have an opportunity to do so, and remind your loved one that there are basically four feelings (mad, sad, glad, and fear) and the rest are variants of these.

This mirroring technique was developed by Carl Rogers after World War II. From the late 1930s to the early 1970s, psychiatry in the United States was dominated by psychoanalysis. To become a trained analyst in the United States in the 1940s one had to complete college, medical school, an internship, and psychiatric residency; go through analysis oneself; and then successfully analyze two patients under supervision. In addition one had to take coursework at a psychoanalytic institute. After World War II it was felt that there would not be enough trained analysts available to treat the many mentally ill requiring their services. Carl Rogers developed an approach known as Rogerian psychotherapy in which therapists with minimal training would rephrase and reflect the patients' statements back to them.

At the time, psychoanalysts had a sick joke about this process. A patient ran into a Rogerian therapist's office and said, "You have got to help me; I am terribly depressed." The Rogerian therapist responded, "You feel a need for professional help because you are so despondent." "Yes, that is correct," exclaimed the patient. "In fact, I am thinking of suicide." "You are so depressed," said the therapist, "that you feel the only way you can gain some control over your pain would be to take your own life." "Exactly," exclaimed the patient. "In fact, I am going to do it right now." The patient then ran over to the therapist's office window and jumped out. The therapist walked to the window and looked down at the street twenty stories below and said, "Splat." Naturally, the highly trained psychoanalysts would look down their noses at individuals with little training who merely rephrased and parroted what patients told them. However, a good many individuals did seem to benefit from this simplified form of therapy, and it is a technique that nearly anyone can employ.

Maintain the "I and Thou" Relationship

A psychiatric resident in the 1960s was confused by the plethora of psychotherapies available and the fact that they all claimed success treating severely ill patients. One Swiss analyst took a female patient with schizophrenia to her house and fed her ice cream, telling her that this was the good mother's milk. Another analyst swore at his patients and physically attacked them. One taught his patients to dance in order to strengthen their ego boundaries. Another had patients act out their childhood conflicts in psychodrama. One analyst specialized in treating schizophrenic males. He demanded no contact between the patient and the family for a year so that the patient could develop transference to the treatment staff. One worked with the family in an effort to treat the "schizophrenogenic mother" and help her see the "double binds" she applied to her children that caused them to become psychotic. Another therapist told a patient, "I never promised you a rose garden." One felt he was schizophrenic himself and chose male attendants to work with his patients whom others felt to be odd and eccentric. The psychiatric resident looked for a common denominator for these widely differing approaches that had reportedly cured patients. His conclusion was that in every case, the author of the treatment modality had stayed with the patient despite a lack of an expression of gratitude or any major sign of improvement. The therapist, in each case, was eager to prove his or her theory and this enabled the individual to stay with the patient for a very long time.

Martin Burber said that the healing element in any form of therapy is the "I and Thou" relationship. The therapist is nonjudging and accepts the patient as a person over an extended period of time. Some of us might also say that the therapist is a conduit of love from a higher power. You are not your partner's therapist and he or she is not yours, but the basic healing element of all therapy can be present in your loving, nonjudgmental, accepting relationship. You can also serve as a conduit for your higher power's love.

Validate and Give Feedback

You may find it useful to use the Rogerian technique as you interact with your ACOA. As you paraphrase and validate your companion's feelings, you are giving her or him a mirror in which to see her or himself. Healthy parents do this for their children. They reflect to the child, "That must have made you angry." "You must have been sad when that happened." "I will wager that made you happy." As a result, the child learns to identify and express her or his feelings. Children in alcoholic homes do not receive this mirroring and learn to suppress their feelings and keep their thoughts to themselves. They have grown up feeling that if they show their feelings, no one will be there to comfort them. In their experience others will walk away or take advantage of them. When ACOAs reach adulthood they frequently have difficulty knowing how they feel and are unable to identify their feelings.

We mentioned Bob and Mary as one of the four examples of shock earlier in this chapter. Mary told us how Bob used this mirroring technique in their relationship and how helpful it was to her. Mary said, "It seemed to me that people thought I was stupid when I was at that party last night." Bob responded, "You feel that people were critical of your intelligence when you were socializing at last night's party." This caused Mary to reflect. "Well, I am not sure if they really were—it might have been a carryover of my childhood and my tendency to be self-critical." Bob then said, "You are not certain if they were really down on you because your perception may have been affected by your childhood experiences." All Bob was doing was rephrasing and reflecting back Mary's own statements so that she could get some distance and think about them. Bob was a trained psychologist and talking in this manner was natural for him. Do not be intimidated by this example, however. This technique was developed for people with little or no training in psychology. No matter what your background, the technique of listening, supporting, and facilitating your adult child's own introspection is one that anyone can utilize. Encourage your adult child to express his or her feelings, and explain that when he or she begins a sentence with "I feel . . . ," your companion will always be right. Your partner can use the same techniques to help you reflect. The process of sharing your mutual reflection results in a stronger and more interesting relationship.

Use "I" Statements

This technique was developed by the late great family therapist Virginia Satir. Her work with families led to work with adult children of alcoholics. Sharon Wegscheider-Cruse, author of *Another Chance* and the founding chairperson of the National Association for Children of Alcoholics, trained under Ms. Satir. Using "I" statements is a way to get your point across without making your partner defensive. Its effectiveness is not limited to a relationship with an ACOA, but it is a helpful tool to use in your relationship.

When you say, "*You* did this" or "*You* failed to do that," it is highly likely that your partner will become defensive and respond negatively to what seems to be an accusation. For example, the wife says to the husband, "You said you were going to pick up the cleaning and you did not do it." The husband is likely to respond, "If you knew how busy I was at the office you would not bring that up," or "You were not doing anything; why didn't you pick it up?" or "What's the big deal—you forgot to get the bread at the grocery store." A way around this defensive impasse is to use an "I" statement. In the example above the wife could begin by saying, "I'm confused." The husband, curious and not threatened, asks, "What are you confused about?" The wife responds, "I thought that I would not be picking up the cleaning today." Her statement is not accusatory and invites further exploration. The husband, now remembering but not feeling threatened, responds, "Oh, I forgot—I said that I would pick it up."

Clarify Needs and Compliments

A common shortcoming in communication occurs when desires aren't clearly expressed in a relationship. For example, when coffee is offered to guests, they need to say if they want sugar or cream in it. If they do not express what they want and drink it black while wishing for cream or sugar, they are unhappy and yet the host cannot correct the problem. In a relationship it is important for each person to tell the other specifically what they would like so that the other person can take action and correct the problem or satisfy the desire. If the husband comes home and the wife says, "Our marriage stinks," or "You do not give me any support," the husband is confronted with an unhappy wife but nothing specific he can do to make it better. If the wife instead tells him, "When you walk in the house without greeting me, grab a beer, and sit in front of the television, it makes me feel that I am not very important to you," the husband can then see how his actions are causing his wife to feel ignored, and he can apologize and take steps to correct the problem in the future. In addition, ask for aid that your partner is capable of giving. For example, stating, "The furnace is not working," or "Our son needs help with his calculus" brings up issues that are probably beyond the average man's ability to fix. Asking your spouse to do things he cannot do will just make him feel inadequate and probably defensive. Requesting tasks he can accomplish has the effect of making him feel useful and needed.

The examples above are of women who need to express their thoughts and desires more directly. In our experience, however, it is the men who have the most difficulty with this. *Men Are from Mars and Women Are from Venus* notes that women like to get out their thoughts and feelings, but do not really want a solution. They want empathy, support, and an attentive listener. Men want to go to their caves and work out their problems in solitude. Talking about thoughts and feelings is a skill that most men have to acquire. If the man is an adult child, it takes even more effort. Men need to make a special effort to tell their spouses what they are thinking and feeling. If one person in a relationship is uncommunicative, the other person uses his or her imagination to try to figure out what the uncommunicative one is thinking and often arrives at conclusions that are much worse than what the quiet person is thinking. In his book *Dave Barry's Complete Guide to Guys*, Dave Barry gives an example of a couple driving along and the man is frowning and silent. The woman thinks, "I wonder if our relationship is progressing too quickly, I wonder if he feels pressured, I wonder if he feels in a corner," and the fellow is thinking, "Damn, the odometer just turned over; I am going to have to change the oil." The woman's misperception of the man's thoughts is likely to lead to some tension in the relationship unless he starts talking to her. Many men are uncomfortable sitting down and talking about thoughts and feelings. They want things to just progress serenely in the relationship without any introspection or discussion. The problem with this is that in any relationship, no matter how blissful, little frustrations and negative feelings are going to come to the surface. Some may be irritating habits of the partner and some may be unconscious patterns of behavior carried over from childhood and projected onto the companion. In any event, if these frustrations are not discussed, they fester and one day the uncommunicative person starts feeling bored with the relationship, sick at the sight of her or his partner, or restless, wanting to get away.

A corollary to this is to clarify when giving a compliment to your partner. "You are the greatest! You are fantastic" are nice statements, but it is even nicer to say specifically what you love about your companion. For example, "The way you went out of your way to help that person shows what a warm and generous person you are. I love you for your kind heart." "The dinner you fixed was really special. You are a fantastic cook and you always present the meal in such an attractive way. You cook with love." These are good techniques for any relationship but are especially important with your adult child. Remember that your partner seldom received compliments as a child, and his or her self-esteem and self-confidence suffered because of this. As an adult your ACOAs may have difficulty accepting compliments, but he or she needs them desperately. Whenever you have an opportunity to give your companion positive feedback, do it. Point out the many nice things your partner does each day and takes for granted. "You certainly have good taste. You have a real knack for decorating." "You must have a green thumb. Your floral arrangements are unbelievable." "You are such a great role model. Our kids are lucky to have you for a parent." When your partner protests, compliment him or her for being humble

and modest as well. It does not cost anything to give your partner positive feedback, but it is worth a great deal to him or her and to your
relationship. Do not forget to occasionally leave a nice card saying how
great your partner is, and send an unexpected floral arrangement once
in a while to express your love and appreciation.

Putting the "Fun" Back in Dysfunction

He who laughs—lasts.

—Alcoholics Anonymous saying

In the previous chapter we discussed the "mind field" of your relationship and some general guidelines as to how you might navigate through it. In this chapter we will talk about how you might employ humor as a tool to dampen the emotional explosions, help your partner not take her or himself so seriously, make yourself more interesting, and make the process of building a relationship more fun. In your relationship, you are both involved in a process of introspection and behavioral change. Laughing at yourselves can make the route more enjoyable. John M. Gottman, coauthor of *The Seven Principles for Making Marriage Work*, notes that in successful, emotionally intelligent marriages the partners demonstrate "repair attempts" to reduce conflict and get the relationship back on track. Humor is restorative if accompanied by a demonstration of your admiration and respect for your partner. We will present a number of examples in which couples used humor to the advantage of their relationships. You probably will want to think up your own techniques, but these samples may provide inspiration for your own imagination.

A NOTE OF CAUTION REGARDING THE USE OF HUMOR

Humor can be helpful in many ways but it is important that you have a relationship in which your partner is assured of your love and respect, and knows that you would never knowingly hurt his or her feelings or belittle him or her in any way. You want your partner to feel good about your joking and teasing and to realize that you want to support his or her efforts to change the patterns of behavior that are getting in the way of experiencing happiness as an adult. It is not fair to tease someone about something that he or she cannot change, and it may increase the person's stress and self-criticism to do so.

YOUR PARTNER COULD BENEFIT FROM SOME CHEER

Adult children tend to be serious. They lack the joie de vivre that people who grew up in loving homes experience. They are frequently on the periphery of social events because they did not learn how to make small talk or to socialize as children. Many parented their parents and could not be spontaneous, emotional, or playful, instead maintaining a façade of control. Their low self-esteem and lack of self-confidence caused them to anticipate rejection and criticism from others. They strove for perfection in an effort to dampen criticism and to feel they could deserve love from others.

Adult children do not like spontaneous events because in their unpredictable childhoods, unexpected events were often traumatic. Holidays and special occasions were disappointing times for them as children and continue to be sources of tension and anxiety for them as adults. You can help your companion learn to have fun in social situations, play games, and enjoy unplanned events, as well as holidays and family celebrations.

No child has an adult inside, but every adult has a child within. You are helping your partner awaken her or his inner child to play, laugh, and cry. Playing and grieving for what they missed in childhood are two of the primary tasks your adult child needs to accomplish to overcome the effects of her or his childhood experiences.

EXAMPLES OF HELPFUL HUMOR IN RELATIONSHIPS

Let us first examine some examples in which humor was used in a positive way to reduce tension and encourage reflection in a relationship. These vignettes may give you some ideas as to how you might attempt to apply humor in your own relationship.

In the preceding chapter, we shared the story of Ted, who was blindsided by Lisa at the French restaurant. He recovered quickly and when Lisa said, "Call me a cab," Ted said, "Okay, you are a cab." This broke the tension and Lisa started laughing. "You are impossible," she said. "Difficult, but not impossible," responded Ted. They were able to laugh together and return to their romantic dinner in the restaurant. Once the tension was broken, they were also able to discuss Lisa's fear that she was becoming too close to Ted and that she would end up being hurt or abandoned by him. She later realized that her angry outburst was really due to her fear of losing Ted and that this behavior could have had the effect of driving him away. Sometimes, when Ted would confront Lisa with her behavior, she would say, "But, but, but . . ." and Ted would tell her, "Now do not try to get away in your motorboat."

Kate and Paul were high school teachers. Kate was the daughter of an alcoholic father, and she shared her childhood experiences and her insight into her adult patterns with her new husband, Paul. They each made an effort to learn about the other's behavioral patterns and try to alter those that caused difficulties in their relationship. They said they decided not to take the process of analyzing their relationship so seriously. As a joke they named Kate's blowups "rage outbursts" (ROs).

Paul said, "If Kate starts having ROs more frequently, I point it out and tell her things must be going pretty well around here." Kate said she could usually laugh when he used this term to describe her outbursts.

Using initials helps to reduce the emotional charge of a topic. The military refers to *WIA*s, *MIA*s, and *KIA*s, which are much less anxiety-provoking terms than *wounded, missing,* and *killed in action.*

Marie was an adult child who was married to a quiet businessman named Henry. She would unconsciously set up situations to confirm that Henry was selfish, like her addicted father and the men she had known in the past. For example, she would leave the dishes in the sink and then think to herself, "He is going to get home from work, walk right past those dishes, and sit in front of the television with a beer." Sure enough, Henry did exactly as she predicted, and Marie then blew up and told him how selfish he was. "You just think of yourself," she screamed. "You leave the dishes for me to do while you go in and have a beer and watch television." When things settled down they discussed what had occurred. Henry said that he would be happy to help out at home, but he was not a psychic. Marie had to admit that had she told Henry she wanted the dishes done, he would have done them and that it was unfair of her to expect him to read her mind. Henry said that from then on whenever Marie tried to put him in the role of being selfish, he would refer to himself as an "SD" (selfish dude). "Oh yeah, I am one of those SDs like your dad and all those schmucks you dated in the past." Marie would laugh, and they would talk about the situation and why she had those feelings. When Marie seemed to be expecting Henry to read her mind, he would bend his head, clasp his hands over his eyes, and say in a tremulous voice, "There is a lady in the front row of the audience with a gold watch." Marie would laugh and say, "Okay—I get it—you are not a mind reader."

Nick and Diane were friends of Henry and Marie. Nick was an adult child of an alcoholic. Diane said that Nick sometimes did the same thing to her and accused her of being selfish and wrapped up in herself. She adopted Henry's abbreviation but modified it to "SB" (selfish babe). Some couples referred to the off-and-on type of relationship that adult children are used to as "RC," or roller-coaster relationships.

Laurie was an adult child who was afraid of flying. She did not have control over the plane and feared that something bad was going to happen. Before the flight Laurie was apprehensive; once on the plane, her anxiety would escalate; and during takeoff, she would grip her husband's arm. Her husband, Joe, would point out that the other passengers were reading or sleeping while she was sitting rigidly, staring out of the window, her eyes glued on the engine, listening for any strange noises or changes in the plane's performance. Laurie would always listen carefully to every word the flight attendant said in the safety lecture and tell Joe to keep quiet when he would try to talk to her while the instructions were given. Joe would agree that it was important for her to listen for the 200th time to the safety instruction. "Out here in the Midwest you need to know the location of your flotation device so you can slip it on before we hit a cornfield." He also told her that the airlines want passengers to attach their seat belts for easier identification of the bodies after a crash.

On one occasion, Laurie and Joe had to take a commuter flight on a small plane. Laurie was confused and upset to find that another couple had taken their assigned seats. "Do not worry about it," Joe said. "We will just take these two empty ones." The seats they took were next to the emergency door. The flight attendant announced, "For those passengers seated by the emergency exits, if anyone does not feel capable of operating the door or assisting in an emergency, please let me know and we will reassign your seats." Laurie started to raise her hand and said, "I don't think . . ." Joe gently pushed her hand down and whispered, "Don't sweat it. If we go down, I am throwing your little butt out first." Laurie started to giggle. Whenever Joe would read about a plane crash, he would tell Laurie, "They found out what caused the plane crash yesterday." "Oh, what was it?" Laurie would ask. He would reply, "The lady who was assigned to watch the engine took her eyes off it for a moment and it went right down."

Joe told Laurie a story about a man who fell off a cliff and was able to grab the branch of a small tree on his way down. As he hung out over the deep precipice he called up to heaven, "Is anyone there?" A thunderous voice came down from the sky, "Yes, this is God." The terrified man asked for help. God replied, "Okay, just let go." The man thinks it over and then yells, "Is there anyone else up there?" Laurie said, "What does that mean—that I am afraid to let go and take a chance?" "Something like that," answered Joe. "Well, I took a chance on you, didn't I?" Laurie smiled. "Well, you got me there," laughed Joe. As mentioned earlier in this chapter, it is important not to tease your partner about something they are unable to control. Some people with panic disorder and fear of flying are unable to control their anxiety and kidding them will not relieve the problem. If you are in doubt about your partner's ability to control his or her anxiety, do not kid your loved one about his or her fears.

Adult children are sensitive to the needs of others but often have difficulty taking care of themselves. Dan was a high school coach who liked to stay in shape. His wife, Wendy, was an adult child. She worked out when they were first married but with the passage of time had neglected her exercise and, at the same time, complained about her weight gain. Dan encouraged her to walk with him in the mornings and she vowed she would, but the next morning she would have an excuse for not getting out of bed. Dan brought a cup of coffee and set it on her nightstand. "I think we'd better start out slow with the exercise," he said. "I am going to read to you about sit-ups today." Each morning he would bring her coffee and read about a different exercise. Wendy laughed but still slept in. The following week he brought coffee and an exercise video and played some of it each morning. Finally, Wendy laughed, "Okay, you win—I am going to get up with you to walk in the mornings." She found she enjoyed the morning walks and their time together, and she was able to drop the pounds she'd gained. "I am usually a bear in the mornings," she said, "but Dan was so cute—he got me up and going without making me mad about it."

When Melissa worried that an item in her refrigerator was spoiled, she would ask Chuck if he thought it was still good. Chuck would tell her to scrape the fungus off it before she prepared it. Melissa worried that her food would be undercooked and repeatedly asked Chuck if he cooked the meat on the grill long enough. He would attempt to reassure Melissa by saying it was "a la Ganges" (the river in India where bodies are placed on burning rafts to be cremated), or he would act worried and say he wasn't sure, that it seemed a little raw to him—just to tease her and get her going.

As we will later discuss in detail, adult children have a need to be in control. Their childhood homes were chaotic and loss of control was associated with bad experiences. As adults, they feel the need to control what they can. Sam said that his wife, Jill, would ask him a question and nonverbally tell him how to answer. She would say (nodding), "Do you think the lawn needs mowing?" Or (turning her head from side to side), "Do you think we want to be looking for a new car now?" Sam said he responded to his ACOA wife's control by answering her in a Caspar Milquetoast voice, saying, "Yes, lambkins," which caused her to laugh and see that she was trying to run the show. Sam told her the Alcoholics Anonymous saying, "If you want to stop spinning your wheels, try getting out of the driver's seat."

Adult children were taught to maintain a front of normalcy for the world when they were growing up. As adults they appear to be calm because they have learned to maintain the appearance of calmness during crisis situations. Your adult child could have just had horribly traumatic things happen to her or him, but if you ask how she or he is, your partner will answer, "Fine." We once introduced an adult child to an ACOA support group, and one of the members of the group looked up at her and said, "How are you doing?" "Fine," the newcomer responded. "Yeah—FINE," answered the veteran group member. "Fouled-up, Insecure, Neurotic, and Enabling." The newcomer blushed but acknowledged that the member had her pegged. The dysfunctional rule to keep the family secrets private, hidden from the outside world, may make it difficult for your partner to discuss childhood experiences. In addition, you will likely find that your companion is upset with you when you talk about seemingly benign present-day family events to persons outside of the family. When Melissa would complain about Chuck's public disclosure of family business, he would imitate the Godfather and say, "Sonny! Never tell anyone outside of the family what you are thinking," which would cause Melissa to smile.

In addition to appearing calm, ACOAs frequently function better than others in stressful situations. Crises were the norm in their childhood experiences and are familiar territory for them. There may be a psychological reason for their calmness as well. During World War II psychiatrists were assigned to the induction centers and men were screened from duty if they were determined to be "neurotic" based on a questionnaire designed by the psychoanalyst Harry Stack Sullivan. When this program was instituted, 100,000 men per month were found to be neurotic. The surgeon general became alarmed, realizing that the country would not be able to muster an army if it deferred that many neurotic men. The word then came down that all men previously determined to be neurotic by the screening would serve. A follow-up study was later done to determine how well the neurotics functioned in battle. To the investigator's surprise it appeared they did better than the nonneurotic soldiers. Further study concluded that the so-called neurotic men had been walking around as civilians with the discomfort of free-floating anxiety and felt helpless to do anything about it. In combat they knew the source of their fear and could take action by shooting back. In the same way your companion is walking around with constant tension, and having a real threat that they can deal with may be a relief to them. (See the rats on the grid experiment described in chapter 5.)

Esther was very sensitive about being ignored or being kept waiting. She had shared with her husband, Robert, that as a child she was often left waiting in the car or on a bar stool drinking a Pepsi while her dad drank with his cronies in the tavern. Robert used this information to tease her when her sensitivity surfaced. "Robert are you still on that computer?" she shouted at her husband in an irritated voice. "Yes, dear, why don't you have yourself a nice cold Pepsi and I will be down in a moment," Robert answered sweetly. "You butt!" yelled Esther, laughing. When Esther would start dwelling on a chronic resentment, Robert would say, "Don't be a hater," or "Did we drink some 'Haterade' this morning?" which would invariably cause Esther to smile and relax.

When Ted would see that Lisa was getting down on herself about something, he would imitate Al Franken's Stuart Smiley character from *Saturday Night Live* and tell her, "Hey, look in the mirror. You're good enough, you're smart enough, and gosh darn it—people like you." Lisa constantly worried about other people's opinions of her. She assumed that they were critical. Ted reminded Lisa that she wasn't running a popularity contest or going for Miss Congeniality and suggested that when she looks at another person, she could just think, "What you think of me is none of my business." Ted said, "Remember what Eleanor Roosevelt said: 'No one can make you feel inferior without your consent.'" On occasion Lisa would become overly self-critical. She would tell herself that she should have had the house spotless or that she ought to have sent out more Christmas cards. Ted would then tell her to "stop 'shoulding' on yourself." Lisa followed Ted's example and started enjoying the use of humor herself. She decided to act out a joke she heard. Ted came home to find Lisa standing nude in front of the full-length mirror in their bedroom. "What are you doing, honey?" Ted asked. "I went to the doctor today, and he told me I had the body of a twenty-year-old." Lisa answered. "Oh yeah?" asked Ted. "What did he say about your forty-year-old butt?" "Your name didn't come up, dear," Lisa said laughing.

Marion was an adult child who tried to be perfect. She'd been a homecoming queen and a model before getting married. Her house had to be perfectly clean. Christmas and other holidays had to be "just so." Her children had to be dressed in name-brand clothing, they had to be groomed, their shoes had to be polished, they had to display good manners. Of course, things never went as Marion hoped, and she was continually frustrated by failing to meet the unrealistic goals she set for herself. Her family was equally frustrated by her demands. The kids complained about their mother's nit-picking criticism. Her husband, Jack, was an easygoing English professor who liked to tease Marion as a way of getting his point across. "We are looking for progress—not perfection," he said. When Marion was stewing about not being able to go out because the house was still a mess, Jack said, "Here's a little poem that might give you something to live by: 'When in worry, when in doubt, run in circles, scream and shout.'" "Oh that's just great," said Marion laughing. "How about this one?" asked Jack. "*Solem mediocres sunt semper in suis optimis.*" "Which means?" asked Marion. "Only the mediocre are always at their best," Jack translated, smiling. "Okay, I get the point—I am driving everyone nuts with my perfectionism," said Marion. "It is not all bad," laughed Jack. "The 'neat freak' of any house is the one who picks up for everyone else. You are saving the rest of us a lot of work—we can count on you to pick up after us." Marion said that Jack referred to her periodic blowups as "a visit from Discordia (goddess of marital strife)."

YOUR PARTNER HAS TWO MAIN TASKS TO ACCOMPLISH

1. Mourn the loss of what they didn't get as children
2. Learn to play and have fun as adults.

As your partner feels secure in the present, he or she is better prepared to put the past in perspective. Your companion can understand why his or her parents acted as they did but cannot go back and obtain what he or she missed as a child. It is helpful for ACOAs to experience the feelings evoked when they accept that they will never receive the unconditional love, nurturance, validation, support, or security they needed as children. These ambiguous losses produce a pessimistic outlook on life. Ted's farewell to Lisa each day as he left for work was "Have a nice day—unless you have other plans."

While the chronic depression and pessimistic outlook are understandable, it isn't helpful for your partner to hold a pity party and blame all the problems and shortcomings of adult life on having been raised in an alcoholic home. Once she or he feels secure in the present, your companion can be thankful for having a loving family and many blessings. The process of revisiting childhood experiences and recalling old feelings is therapeutic. Analyzing current behavioral patterns and changing those that may be causing problems in your relationship marks further growth and improvement. However, it is not necessary and is often counterproductive to dwell on the traumas of the past. As Professor Jack told Marion, "The wise man has many cuts, the happy man doesn't count the scars." He advised her to focus on today by saying, "Yesterday is history, tomorrow is unknown, and today is a gift—that is why they call it the present."

The process of positive change requires constant attention from both of you and daily effort to maintain and further improve your relationship. It does not have to be work; in fact, much of the time it can be fun. The process is easier if you do not take it too seriously. In time you will get to know each other's adult patterns of behavior and can point out when your partner is repeating some childhood defensive act that is inappropriate for the adult situation. Kidding each other can lighten things up and help you and your companion to relax and laugh at yourselves. When Marion was "cranked up" on an issue and started to shout, her husband, Jack, would make a cranking motion with his hands and quote the following anticlastic phrase by Ben Franklin: "Your argument is sound, nothing but sound." When Marion would feel the pressure of time and a sense of urgency, Professor Jack would quote Groucho Marx: "Time flies like an arrow, fruit flies like bananas."

THE PUSH-PULL OF COMMITMENT AND TRUST

Marriages are made in heaven—but so are thunder and light-ening.

—ANONYMOUS

Your relationship started out rapidly and smoothly. Everything was going well until you ran into an emotional explosion that blind-sided you. You gave your partner a hug, expressed your love, and told your partner that the explosion was her or his problem. Later, you dis-cussed the situation and arrived at a mutual understanding of the sensi-tive area that produced the blowup. As the relationship continued, you began to see a pattern of things going smoothly followed by an explo-sion. It was not always possible to discover the area of sensitivity in your partner's background that triggered the emotional outburst. Sometimes your partner talks about your having an argument and making up, and you can't remember having a dispute. Once again, you find yourself confused about the relationship.

To understand this phenomenon, we need to review your companion's childhood experiences and how your companion unconsciously reproduced his or her childhood environment in adult life. This is what psychoanalysts used to call repetition compulsion, where the individual is unconsciously compelled to repeat the patterns of behavior he or she developed in childhood.

Your partner grew up in a home where the atmosphere was determined by the disease of alcoholism. As a child your companion did not know what was going to happen next; there was no continuity and no predictability. The only certainty was that there would be a crisis. The parent would pass out, lose her or his job, get arrested, get in an accident, become abusive, set fire to the house, give away the pet, cause embarrassment, break promises, and fight with her or his spouse. Alcoholic binges and inappropriate behavior were frequently followed by remorse and promises to do better.

As a child your companion assumed that all families lived with this kind of unpredictable, unstable home life. Children tend to generalize and think that all kids share the same experiences at home that they do. Dr. Peter Fleming, director of the Menninger Adult Hospital, once told how his family bought Fleming coffee, and his children assumed that all families had their names on their coffee cans. When your partner was a child, she or he may have visited the nonalcoholic homes of friends and relatives and enjoyed being there, but did not understand the reason that the atmosphere was different from their home.

As a teenager your companion vowed that her or his future home would be different, envisioning a rose-covered cottage with a picket fence, where peace and harmony would reign and the bluebird of happiness would sing at the window. There would be no drinking in her or his future home. Despite this idyllic image, your partner still had an unconscious attraction to "exciting" individuals who turned out to be addicted, impulsive, and immature. This is eros, the all-consuming, obsessive, passionate relationship that involves struggle, obstacles to overcome, and a willingness to endure suffering for the sake of the relationship. The relationship is exciting, dramatic, and constantly disappointing. Arousing and being aroused produce the excitement that sparks the eros relationship. The mysterious partner would suddenly fail to show up and fail to call. There would be a blowup that sometimes was abusive and then a period of remorse and making up. These roller-coaster, off-and-on relationships were chaotic and unhappy, but familiar. Having gone through a childhood where feelings were suppressed, the pain and excitement of uncertainty and disappointment helped the ACOA feel alive. After going through several of these exciting but unhappy relationships and attaining some degree of emotional maturity and experience, some ACOAs are able to realize that they are repeating a childhood pattern and that their relationship problems are due to internal rather than external factors. They then make a conscious decision to seek another type of love, which the Greeks called agape. This is a partnership in which a loving couple is deeply committed. They share core values and interests, and they support one another's growth as individuals. Partners in this type of relationship trust and respect one another, seek serenity and security in their relationship, and are friends as well as lovers. This is a deep, comfortable relationship based on openness and trust wherein the individuals share everything about themselves and still love each other. It is this knowing and being known that produces the excitement in an agape relationship. The desire for agape love has motivated your partner to seek a committed relationship with you.

COMMITMENT IS SCARY AND DIFFICULT FOR YOUR PARTNER

Constructive commitment is basic to a good relationship. It is the glue that holds your partnership together. It is also one of the most problematic aspects of your union for your companion. Like so many aspects of adult living, your adult child lacked exposure to a healthy committed relationship growing up. Their parents may have stuck together in an unhappy, abusive, codependent relationship, but this was not a healthy commitment. They stayed together, not out of love, but due to the external admonitions of the church and the community or for fear of not being able to make it financially or emotionally on their own. The parents may have added to your partner's guilt by telling them that they stayed in an unhappy relationship "for the children." The children may have been praying that the parents would separate. The nonaddicted parent was frequently a codependent enabler. That is, the nonaddicted parent was totally focused on the addict and ignored his or her own feelings and wishes. The codependent's mood was dependent upon the addict's mood, and he or she was preoccupied with trying to "fix" the addict's problem. Many marriages between an addicted person and a codependent seem to be ironclad, while a good many others totally lack commitment. Infidelity and a readiness to break the covenant on a moment's notice characterize the latter fragile unions. The addicted parent may suddenly leave the family, or the codependent may take the children and leave the addict.

Adult children tend to think in terms of black-and-white extremes. Their idea of a committed relationship tends to be like their parents' "until death do us part" or avoiding commitment at all costs. It is unlikely that your partner was exposed to a constructively committed relationship. In addition to lacking healthy committed role models to imitate, your partner has many reasons to fear commitment.

Commitment requires trust. Your partner may have encountered few trustworthy individuals in her or his past. Trust implies making oneself vulnerable, open, honest, dependable, loyal, faithful, and feeling emotionally safe. Adult children tend to be loyal but have difficulty with the other aspects of trust. Your companion's low self-esteem causes her or him to feel unworthy and unlovable, and your partner suspects that anyone who loves her or him must also have serious problems. Your ACOA is not used to having anyone consistently there for her or him and may become increasingly anxious, anticipating that you will eventually abandon her or him. In addition, your adult child may have a warped view of commitment, fearing that it entails being controlled by you, accepting a huge burden for the remainder of her or his life, and losing her or his identity and independence in the relationship. Your partner may be concerned about having to take care of you the way she or he looked after her or his parents while growing up. The first time your adult child encounters a problem, she or he may have the urge to run from the relationship. This urge is further encouraged by our disposable society that makes people think they should be happy all of the time, and if there are problems with the relationship, they can just get rid of it and find a new one.

Greg was an independent businessman who was divorced from his first wife. He was a recovering alcoholic. During his childhood Greg's mother had been hospitalized several times with a diagnosis of schizophrenia, and his father had been preoccupied with the mother's illness and supporting the family. Greg met Charlotte through Alcoholics Anonymous. She was a salesperson who had also been previously married. Charlotte was an adult child and a recovering alcoholic. Their relationship was rocky because of difficulties with trust and commitment on both their parts. Greg said that he tried to remain on good terms with his ex-wife for his children's sake, but Charlotte would blow up if he was merely polite to his former spouse and felt that he should show absolute loyalty to her. She wanted them to have a permanent relationship and a blended family but, again, blew up when he proposed bringing the children with them on a date because, she said, "They would be imposing on my time with you." Greg said he had difficulty with commitment and his gut, unspoken response was, "Screw you. I do not need anyone trying to control me—hit the road." The relationship was stuck in this off-and-on-again impasse. Intellectually, Charlotte knew that to move forward she would have to trust Greg and not demand that he constantly prove he was devoted to her alone. In the same way, Greg knew that for the relationship to progress he needed to be committed and not ready to throw in the towel every time Charlotte became angry or demanding. Both are aware of the patterns they need to change to have a good relationship but neither is able to let go of those childhood patterns. As a result they continue the pattern of mistrust, blowup, abandonment, then passionate reconciliation that they have been in for the past several years. Neither is happy with the situation, but it is the roller-coaster type of relationship that is familiar to both of them.

Your adult child wants a close loving relationship but has never experienced a committed relationship of this nature. He or she is used to the off-and-on roller-coaster relationship experienced with the alcoholic parent and previous relationships. As a result your partner may, unconsciously, establish a push-pull, on-and-off relationship with you or perceive your relationship to be this type of union.

COMMITMENT IS THE GLUE THAT HOLDS A GOOD RELATIONSHIP TOGETHER

The quality relationship you both want is not possible without the assurance that you are going to stay with each other through good times and bad. It is the cement that holds the other elements of your relationship together. You want to trust each other completely, and you are both committing yourselves to the values you both hold dear in life. God, family, friends, doing nice things for others, and your relationship with your partner are the top priorities in your life.

WHAT IS CONSTRUCTIVE COMMITMENT?

A constructively committed relationship is based on truth and honesty. Dependability is extremely important. If you say you will do something, do it, and if you say you are going to be somewhere, be there. Of course, in this type of relationship you are faithful and loyal to one another. There is mutual respect for one another as individuals, and you give each other support in your efforts to develop and use your talents to the extent of your potential. Humor isn't an absolute requirement, but it helps keep a relationship vital and it reduces stress. Sometimes you depend on your partner and sometimes they depend on you. Sometimes there is intimacy and sometimes more detachment when you focus on individual goals and activities. Being flexible and keeping a balance in your relationship maintains the vital dynamic quality of your life together.

In the words of Hemingway, "Love is to want to do things for." If you have a constructive commitment, you do not have to make an effort to do little kind favors for your partner—you want to do them. You want to be committed for the sake of your children. Your religion encourages you to keep your covenant with your higher power and with one another. A committed relationship strengthens the partnership in times of adversity, and feelings of safety and security are engendered by your committed relationship.

ACOAs fear anger, including their own. They are black-and-white thinkers. They think, "If I am angry, I do not love you, and if you are angry, you do not love me." They may set up a situation to justify their negative feelings, saying something like "You do the yard work *now* or I am out of here" as Mandy said to Ralph in chapter 2. Or, they may build a case to support their fear that you will abandon them for someone else. In chapter 3 we described how Marie set Henry up to be an SD (selfish dude) by letting him walk by the dishes and then accusing him of only caring about himself. This is an example of an adult child unconsciously attempting to repeat a childhood pattern, justifying her perception of the current relationship as if it was the same off-and-on type of relationship she'd had before.

Rachel was a secretary who married her boss, Norman. Norman reported that Rachel would approach him in a very passionate manner and then suddenly, for no apparent reason, she would be cold and distant. When he attempted to approach her, she would become angry and say, "That is all you want from me isn't it? Your own selfish sexual pleasure." To Rachel's surprise, Norm did not react in an angry manner. He remained calm and expressed his confusion about the change in Rachel's behavior but did not push the issue. Later, as they discussed this pattern, Rachel could see that she was unconsciously repeating the off-and-on relationships she had known in the past.

Frank was an adult child who was his family's "hero." His hard work and attention to detail were personality traits that led to his becoming a successful independent businessman. He married Leslie, a legal secretary, and showered her with expensive gifts. She quit her job because Frank wanted her to be a stay-at-home mom. Leslie was shocked when she purchased some items for herself and Frank hit the ceiling. "Do you think I am made of money?" he shouted. "Is that why you married me—so you could use me for money?" She did not fight back or protest but let Frank calm down. When they were eventually able to discuss the event quietly, Frank could see that he was unconsciously setting up the type of relationship he had known in the past in which he felt exploited by others. Once this phenomenon is recognized and discussed in your relationship, it will be easier to identify when it comes up again. Eventually, your adult child will be able to catch him- or herself before reacting and talk about his or her unconscious tendency to establish the old, familiar pattern of behavior.

For this reaction to occur, your partner may not actually set up a situation that repeats the pattern; she or he may simply perceive the pattern where it does not exist. For example, Jim was a landscape architect who had fallen in love with a physical therapist named Cathy, who was an adult child of an alcoholic. After they had been married for some time, Jim asked Cathy if she wanted to go to a movie. Cathy said no, she would rather stay home and watch television. They made love that night. The next day Cathy remarked that it was great the way they had fought and then made up. Jim was confused. "When did we fight?" he asked. "You remember, you wanted to go to a movie and I said no and you were mad, but then you made up when we went to bed." Jim said, "I was not mad—I was just giving you a choice." "Oh, yes, you were—and now here we are fighting again," said Cathy. As they discussed both incidents, Cathy began to see that a difference of opinion was not the same as a fight. She acknowledged that saying no was difficult for her, and on the rare occasions when she did, she usually felt guilty afterward, thinking she had hurt the other person by not going along with her or his wishes. Cathy was also able to talk about her past off-and-on relationships in which she would fight and then make up. "I know I do that," she said. "Sometimes I pick a fight so we can make up afterward." "Let me know when you think we are fighting," Jim laughed.

By *commitment* we mean that you both give time, energy, and attention to the relationship. You remain together because of love and respect for each other. Some codependent partners feel they must "stand by their man," as Tammy Wynette sang, come hell or high water. However, our society promotes the concept of disposable relationships. This is a feel-good society where everyone is supposed to be happy all of the time. If the relationship is no longer gratifying, then get rid of it and move on to one that is. There is a tendency in society and among some adult children to run from commitment when things get tough.

In a healthy commitment there is a balance of intimacy and detachment that allows each partner to grow as an individual. There is respect for one another's boundaries. Partners stay in the relationship during times of adversity but think enough of themselves to leave it if they feel abused and their companion shows no desire to change.

Adult children both fear and want a committed relationship for a number of reasons. In a committed relationship they feel vulnerable to being hurt or abandoned and are concerned that commitment might mean being eternally burdened with a tremendous obligation. In a committed relationship the adult child cannot always have his or her way, which produces anxiety about losing control. Adult children feel unlovable and unworthy and they think, "If someone loves me, that person must be flawed." While the eros type of love caused them pain and recreated the unhappy relationship they had with their addicted parent, it was familiar, it made them feel alive, and it was not perceived as being as boring as the safe and secure agape relationship appeared to be. However, they want a lifelong, trusting, loving relationship. A good relationship results in more time and energy to focus on other goals in life, while personal growth and a deepening of the partnership itself can take place within the security of a committed relationship. Trust develops from a committed relationship with a safe partner.

Your ACOA does not know what to reasonably expect from a relationship. In a good relationship, the partners negotiate and compromise disagreements. You can help your partner by talking about disagreements and how to resolve them. It will be difficult your adult child to identify and share her or his feelings. Norm told his ACOA partner, Rachel, "Sure you feel that way. I see things differently—but that is okay. It is good for us as a couple when you let me know what your feelings are. It's the sharing that makes us closer." Norm validated Rachel's feelings and helped her name her feelings. "You must have felt angry when you thought I was ignoring you." "You must feel good about yourself after receiving all those compliments on the dinner you prepared last night." "You were angry thinking that I was paying more attention to Susan than to you at the party." Validation does not mean that you agree, but it does mean respect for similarities and differences of feelings.

Your companion has difficulty with confrontation. When there is conflict your ACOA tends to become fearful and feels like running. As they say in Alcoholics Anonymous, FEAR equals "forget everything and run." Adult children tend to feel that anything that goes wrong is their fault. Jim said that he discussed with Cathy these tendencies and their impact on the relationship. Jim said that when they disagreed on a topic, he told Cathy, "Why don't we take a look at this no matter who is right or wrong. We are both good people and we love each other, but we need to figure out what is going wrong here." Jim reported that they practiced problem solving as a couple and, eventually, were able to sit down and have a reasonable discussion when conflict arose between them. Frequently, there are differences of opinion that cannot be resolved or compromised. These can be recognized as areas were you each think differently and accepted as such. For example, one of you may have been raised Catholic and the other Protestant. It is not necessary that one of you convert to the other's religion in order to get along as a couple. Even Republicans and Democrats have been known to cohabit peacefully together.

COMMIT 100 PERCENT TO YOUR PARTNER BUT BE CAPABLE OF RENEGOTIATING IF CIRCUMSTANCES CHANGE

This relationship is one of your priorities in life, and you want to give yourself 100 percent to making it the best it can be for the rest of your lives together. This does not mean sacrificing your needs or your boundaries for your partner, but it does mean that the relationship is important to you and you will pay attention to it daily and put it before less important priorities in your life.

If your partner becomes abusive or addicted or demonstrates intolerable behaviors, you may need to renegotiate the relationship. This means discussing with your partner the changes you have observed that you cannot live with. If your partner is unable or unwilling to change these behaviors, then you must think about breaking the commitment and ending the relationship. No one should have to tolerate verbal, much less physical, abuse. It also means that you recognize what are your own problems that you may be able to fix and what are your partner's patterns that you cannot alter. You also recognize that your happiness and unhappiness are not dependent on your partner's mood.

AN EXAMPLE OF UNHEALTHY COMMITMENT

As we have seen, adult children are full of surprises. From your experience you might expect that your partner would run out the door the first time he or she felt mistreated, but until your companion gained some insight into his or her adult patterns, he or she probably put up with all sorts of abuse rather than face being abandoned by a significant other.

Mary Jo was a middle-aged housewife who presented herself as a psychiatric emergency at two o'clock in the morning, stating that she could not take her home situation any longer. She said, "My husband came home drunk, and he vomited on the floor. Then he threw the baby against the wall. He pushed me down. Then he laughed and said I was ugly and no wonder he had to have a drink. I told him to be careful not to break my mother's china and he took it and smashed it. Then he told me that he'd had sex with my sister and that he had told everyone in town about it." The psychiatric resident was carefully taking notes and noting empathetically as the woman tearfully related the trauma she had experienced. "And then you decided to come to the hospital for help?" he inquired. "No, that was fifteen years ago. The next thing that happened was . . ." The young physician was shocked to learn that she had fifteen years of these horror stories of abuse. He then asked the obvious question, "Why do you stay in this relationship?" "Because I love him," Mary Jo replied. "Have you ever considered divorce?" The resident queried. "I do not believe in divorce," the woman replied. This is an extreme, but unfortunately not rare, example of a codependent, masochistic woman married to a nonrecovering alcoholic. It is certainly a committed relationship, but not a constructively committed one.

Surprisingly, many ACOAs remain loyal to their abusive spouses because they fear change. Most people, no matter what their childhood experiences, avoid change because it is the unknown. They figure that the ruts they've gotten into in life may not be the happiest, but they are familiar, while making a change would put them into unfamiliar and therefore frightening circumstances. Frequently, it is the controlling spouse who makes the decision to leave and forces the ACOA to make a change. We have seen many ACOAs over the years who said they prayed that God would preserve their marriage and not let their spouse leave them, and later in life, the same individuals said how happy they were that those prayers were not answered as they wished. Looking back over their lives they realize that being forced out of their unhappy ruts was the best thing that could have happened. Of course, if the change is not accompanied by introspection and self-awareness, they will find another abusive mate to continue the unhappy childhood patterns that are familiar to them.

Ellen was the daughter of an abusive, alcoholic, and distant narcissistic mother. She married a man who she later described as a combination of both of her parents. "At times he was physically abusive. I shook my finger at him, and he grabbed my arm and dislocated my shoulder. On another occasion he broke my nose and blackened both of my eyes. I tried to deny that he was having affairs, but I was finally forced to acknowledge that he had not been faithful to me from the beginning of our marriage. He constantly told me that I was 'stupid' and 'crazy.'" Ellen was an intelligent woman who, at times, appeared to have insight into herself and her relationship. But her fear of abandonment overwhelmed her when her husband made the decision to leave her. "I guess he was right about being 'crazy' because I continued to tell myself that I loved him. When he finally told me he did not love me and was getting a divorce, I was frightened to death. I told him that he did love me. I begged him to stay and admitted that I spent too much of the money he gave me. I should not have blown up and talked back to him. I said I was sorry for getting the order of protection because I knew it would make him mad."

THE BEST OF BOTH WORLDS

Your partner decided that she or he no longer wanted the passionate, obsessive, off-and-on relationships that repeated her or his childhood paradigm. Instead, your ACOA made a rational decision to seek a committed, trusting, secure, and safe relationship with you, though this type of relationship seemed boring to them in the past. You can help your companion enjoy the best of both types of love. Knowing your partner and being known are the primary sources of excitement in an agape relationship. Your humor is a way to keep your partner excited and interested since it relies on surprise, adding excitement and spice to the relationship. Initially you will want to make things predictable for your partner to help them feel safe and secure in your relationship. Later, the introduction of spontaneity and good surprises will add positive excitement to your partnership. Having separate interests and encouraging your partner to develop his or her own unique talents and skills will, at first, cause some anxiety as your adult child will fear that you are rejecting her or him. Disagreements and negotiating differences of opinion will likewise produce anxiety initially but, in the long run, will lead to a healthy relationship.

As you are able to discuss your childhood experiences and the patterns of behavior you developed that now affect your adult lives, you will experience a deepening of your relationship. You will experience the good feeling that comes from loving someone who knows everything about you and still loves you. Hopefully you entered this relationship being happy on your own—you were able to support yourself, live alone, and be happy with yourself and your life—and you did not get into this relationship because you were lonely, because your friends were getting married, because you needed someone, or because you were looking for someone to make you feel whole or to bring you happiness. It is not your job to make your partner happy nor is it your partner's job to make you happy. Similarly, your companion's unhappiness should not cause you to be unhappy. You can empathize, but remember that your partner's problems are his or her own and your problems are your own. Love cannot be forced or coerced; it can only be freely given. Your partner will come to recognize that you are in the relationship by choice rather than need or compulsion. It is wonderful to have a committed relationship in which you love each other unconditionally. In this type of relationship, it does not matter how you are feeling at any given moment—happy, scared, depressed, or angry—you always know that you love your partner and vice versa. When you know you are loved unconditionally by a person you love, you have an understanding of the nature of God or your higher power and the love he has for us. In the long run, the deep, committed, agape relationship offers more passion and positive excitement than the roller-coaster eros relationship ever could, while remaining secure, safe, and serene.

THE PARADOX OF
CHRONIC TENSION

Alcoholics are not all alike. Some start drinking in grade school, whereas others do not have a problem until late in life. Some drink every day, some drink in binges. Some drink beer or wine and others drink hard liquor. In the same way, adult children of alcoholics have different childhood experiences and sustain different types of trauma. Their personalities vary, and they grew up at different stages of the family's history with alcohol. The children in such homes may have assumed different roles within the family in their efforts to cope with stress. Their experiences also likely depended on the parent's stage of addiction during the child's formative years. Despite the variations in their childhood experiences, ACOAs are all tense as adults.

People who have not grown up in homes with alcoholic parents often underestimate the amount of stress experienced by those who have. In many cases, their anxiety was at the level associated with sweaty palms, elevated heart rate, diarrhea, and the fear of dying. Think about how it would feel to have someone stick a gun in your face—this is the level of fear that many adult children carry with them.

Some researchers feel that adult children suffer from post-traumatic stress disorder and that the traumatic experiences they sustained as children are on the level of war-time stresses that soldiers endure. These researchers point out that as adults, many of these children are overly alert, psychically numbed, and constantly tense.

It is important to recognize the degree of anxiety and tension these people experience because common tension-relieving activities such as taking a hot bath or going for a walk are about as effective as using a BB gun to hunt elephants.

Paradoxically, adult children can appear to be unusually calm in times of crisis, and many succeed in crisis-oriented fields such as emergency health care, the military, or law enforcement. The fact that they appear to function calmly in these positions can make it easy to discount the possibility that they suffer from constant tension. However, this behavior reflects being raised in a tension-filled home in which there were periodic crises. In such homes, the children become acclimated to emergency situations and learn to view normal situations as the interval preceding the next impending crisis. Children of alcoholics learn to bury their feelings and put on a front of well-being. They grew up maintaining a façade of normalcy to the outside world while their home was in chaos. As adults they continue to maintain this calm front during times of stress. If you ask adult children how things are going, most will answer "fine"—no matter what stresses they have been experiencing in their lives. Ironically, when you see that an adult child is anxious, it probably means that things are going well in his or her life and relationship with you.

Ann described what it was like growing up in her alcoholic home. A young woman who somewhat resembled the actress Anjelica Huston, she appeared to be a self-confident businesswoman. She said her childhood home was filled with tension in which nothing was secure. The only thing that her family knew for sure was that there would be another crisis. They did not discuss it, but all lived with the constant, underlying tension that another unpredictable event would soon disrupt their lives. In her words, "I grew up worrying what was going to happen next." Her father was in several automobile accidents and was cited by the police for driving while under the influence. Even after his driver's license was suspended, he continued to drive when he had been drinking. Ann was in constant fear that he would be killed in an accident or arrested.

Ann's father was often mean and destructive when he came home, and Ann would worry whether her parents would fight upon his arrival. Sometimes her father actually struck her mother, and although she wanted to protect her mother, Ann feared that her father would then hit her as well. Sometimes Ann's father blamed his stress on her mother or the children. Ann's brothers typically would seclude themselves in their rooms. Although she suspected that they were also frightened, the children did not talk about it.

Another problem adding to Ann's insecurity was her father making major decisions about family life without consulting other members. Sometimes he would blatantly lie about such matters to cover up his responsibility. One day, Ann and her siblings came home from school and learned that their dog was gone. Her father claimed that the dog must have ran away, but later they heard him tell their mother that he had given the dog away. According to Ann, "We never knew what might happen next."

Ann also had to live with the prospect of embarrassment outside of the home. Her older brother played high school football, and she was a cheerleader. Her father would come to the games drunk and yell at them. Sometimes he would get into fights. One time, he vomited on himself and then passed out right in front of the bleachers. Ann cleaned him up and, with the assistance of her friends, helped him to the car. She experienced deep shame. She once tried to tell her father how embarrassing his behavior was for her. He responded, "I am not trying to win a G.D. popularity contest."

On a superficial level, it is easy to understand why Ann would be tense as a child. The atmosphere in her childhood home was filled with tension. Her father was aggressive toward other people as well as self-destructive, and the crises he caused were unpredictable. A dependent child in that environment would fear for their own safety as well as the safety of the other family members. Closer examination of Ann's childhood experience reveals that Ann felt responsible for her father's irrational behavior and blamed herself for her inability to keep him from drinking. Her family's unspoken rules were typical of an addicted family. As Claudia Black described in her book *It Will Never Happen to Me*, the rules were "don't talk, don't trust, and don't feel." They were isolated from one another and experienced inner tension that couldn't be expressed or validated. They were expected to put up a front of normalcy to the outside world.

At the deepest level there is something not immediately apparent from Ann's story. She experienced the ambiguous loss of parental love. While most children take their parents' unconditional love for granted, Ann received neither the attention nor the support that are essential to developing a sense of security. As a result, Ann's underlying insecurity weakened her ability to cope with the stress present in her childhood home.

WHAT YOU CAN DO TO HELP

One thing that can be done to reduce the tension associated with an ACOA's chronic anxiety is to encourage or even facilitate measures that directly mitigate the symptoms of tenseness. The most commonly recommended methods of reducing the physical symptoms are generally not potent enough to relieve the pervading tension experienced by the typical adult child, but they can be of some value when used in conjunction with other approaches.

Therapists would probably disagree as to which relaxation methods were superficial and which were intermediate in strength. Hot baths, massages, and deep breathing can help, as can relaxation techniques such as progressively tightening muscles and then relaxing them in groups. Some individuals are able to obtain greater states of repose by listening to music, using visualization, and even sitting in a hot tub. Exercise can become a healthy addiction and is an excellent outlet for frustration and anger. At sufficiently high levels, it can have some antidepressant effects. Meditation, if practiced regularly, can also lead to relaxation. There are many books and groups that teach methods of meditation but probably the easiest way is simply to sit in a relaxed manner, breathe in through the nose to the diaphragm, and exhale through the mouth while concentrating on counting the breaths.

When you experience a distracting thought or feeling, just try to make note of it as a distraction and go back to counting your breaths. Prayer is another form of meditation that can be comforting and relaxing.

The reason that the superficial and intermediate methods of relieving tension do not provide long-term relief to adult children is that they do not address the underlying insecurity that permeates their view of the world. It has been shown that if you put a laboratory rat on a grid and shock him periodically, he will develop symptoms of stress. If you give the rat a lever that will stop the shock, the rat will constantly press the lever and no stress symptoms will develop. If you then randomly shock the rat, regardless of whether he presses the lever, the rat will develop stress. Establishing a consistent, predictable routine and a loving, secure environment for your partner will reduce some of her or his tension over time. Of course, your partner is not used to consistency and will react with a sense of dread absent additional assurances. A calm, predictable milieu is abnormal for adult children, so do not be surprised if initially your partner becomes more anxious and attempts to create or perceive a crisis to reestablish the chaotic environment she or he is used to. Stay cool. Your calmness will have a reassuring effect on your loved one. Eventually, the predictable routine will reduce their tension.

Help your partner see that things have changed in his or her life. Encourage your ACOA to count his or her blessings and point out how the present environment differs from his or her childhood home. Initially, you will want to give your partner a feeling of being in control. Start by giving them choices. "Would you rather have dinner at six or seven?" "Would you prefer to go to the movie or stay home tonight?" Adult children don't like spontaneous, unplanned events because they remind them of the unpredictable crises they experienced during childhood. As your partner's tension lessens and he or she feels more in control, you may want to introduce little surprises such as a loving card left by your partner's toothbrush or in the car, an un-birthday present, flowers for no particular reason, or a spontaneous night out and later perhaps a vacation trip. These spontaneous acts help your partner see that while life isn't predictable, unexpected events can be a good thing.

It's always a good idea to emphasize a person's strengths before pointing out a weakness. Norman Vincent Peale used to refer to the "sandwich approach." You give a compliment, point out a problem, and then finish up with another positive statement about the person. It is an effective way to tell your loved one information that she or he does not want to hear about her or himself. Your partner is sensitive to criticism and needs to know that you speak from love; your message won't get through if you are perceived as being judgmental.

Use humor to help your adult child (see chapter 3, "Putting the 'Fun' Back in Dysfunction"). If your partner appears nervous, point it out and say that this must mean things are going pretty well for him or her. Stacy was an adult child who said, "Worry is my middle name." Her husband, Chris, calmed her down by agreeing with her and exaggerating her apprehension to a ridiculous degree. Stacy would say, "We had a beautiful summer, but we will probably pay for it in the winter." Chris would respond, "Oh my, we had better start buying provisions right now and stock up for the blizzards! How about getting a generator to use when the electricity goes off? Maybe we should get some sled dogs and train them so we can get to the store when the roads are blocked." It helped Stacy laugh and see how silly she was to assume that since we had a nice summer the winter would be bad. Behavioral therapists call this technique "flooding." Instead of trying to reassure the patient, they give the person his or her worst fears in a magnified form.

Let your partner talk to you about her or his childhood experiences. It is easier to do this when you are working together in the garden or on some project around the house. Your partner will recognize that talking openly about childhood thoughts and feelings will immediately reduce some of the tension she or he is experiencing. As your companion shares some childhood experiences and feelings, you will naturally think of your own formative years. Share your memories and feelings with your partner. This will encourage the dialogue between you; help you humbly realize that nearly everyone, including you, experiences dysfunction during childhood; and deepen your mutual understanding.

For example, Betty was an emergency-room nurse who reported that her husband, Louis, was helpful to her in her efforts to reduce her anxiety as an adult. She could remember very little about her childhood and did not like to think or talk about those times in her life. With her husband's encouragement, she remembered staying awake all night as a child, worrying about her alcoholic father drinking in the local taverns. She recalled that she sat in her bed at night praying that her dad would arrive home safely. When she finally heard his footsteps on the porch, she would pray that her parents wouldn't fight. As an adult she learned that her brother and sisters had been in their rooms praying as well, but as kids, they did not talk to each other about their dad's drinking, much less about their feelings at the time. By morning Betty was tired and frequently sick. Looking back, she thought she was probably worn out from worry. Betty liked to stay home from school and watch *Leave it to Beaver, I Love Lucy,* and *Father Knows Best* and pretend that the TV families were her family. She played with paper dolls, and the artificial families she created were always very loving.

As an adult Betty said that her fellow workers thought she was calm and competent as an emergency-room nurse, but she always felt on edge internally. She met a husky emergency medical technician (EMT) who was a teetotaler. Betty, like many female adult children, was attracted to men who appeared big and strong because she felt safe with them. Louis seemed polite and gentle and she felt secure with him. They married and had a good relationship, but Betty became increasingly anxious. She talked openly with Louis about her childhood feelings and what she intellectually knew about the patterns of behavior associated with adult children of alcoholics. She knew she was a good emergency-room nurse and that she could remain calm and clearheaded in times of crisis, and she thought this was because she had grown up facing and dealing with stressful situations. Louis identified with many of her adult patterns of behavior. His parents weren't drinkers but his mother had bouts of mental illness, and the family never knew when she was going to be ill and either confined to her bedroom or in the hospital for weeks and sometimes months on end. Louis said it was frightening for him as a child, and he worried that she might die during one of these episodes. He took on many of the responsibilities at home, looking after his younger siblings, housecleaning, cooking, and nursing his mother. He thought that these experiences influenced him to become a caretaker as an adult and resulted in his becoming an EMT.

Louis did a number of positive things to help Betty. He listened empathetically and shared painful memories from his own life that were similar to Betty's. By opening up to Betty, Louis was making himself vulnerable to her, demonstrating that he had also experienced trauma as a child and that he, too, had patterns in his adult life he needed to examine and perhaps change. This made it easier for Betty to talk about her past and to express her feelings about her childhood. Louis knew he could not make up for the losses Betty experienced as a child, but he could provide her with another source of unconditional love. He bought Betty a puppy that delighted her. The unannounced, spontaneity of the gift was good in that it helped Betty see that surprises and unexpected events can be positive. Louis was deconditioning her negative response to unscheduled happenings. Life isn't predictable, and Louis was helping Betty anticipate the mystery of life with less dread. An unexpected benefit of puppy ownership resulted when Betty took the dog to obedience training class. She said she learned her dog was more secure when she took charge and set the rules. She said it helped her realize she needed to do this with her children as well.

In the example above, Betty did not resolve the underlying insecurity that was caused by the ambiguous loss of a close emotional relationship with her parents. This is a problem that she and Louis will want to address at some point. This loss is more difficult to recognize and will take months and probably years to resolve. Your partner may eventually recognize that he or she missed out on the unconditional love and support from parents that most children experience. No one can go back and have his or her parents be different. The only realistic solution is to experience the loss and accept the fact that the relationship he or she wanted was not there and never will be. No one in the present can make up for this loss, either. As the individual mourns this loss over time, he or she will feel more settled and secure in him- or herself.

DEALING WITH TENSENESS AT INAPPROPRIATE TIMES

Remember Pavlov's dogs? This was a classic experiment in behavioral psychology that demonstrated "conditioning." The dogs were conditioned by ringing a bell when they were fed. Soon ringing the bell alone would cause them to salivate. Children in alcoholic homes are similarly conditioned to associate events such as holidays and meal times with traumatic experiences. As a result, in their adult lives, they may become anxious on occasions that most people would see as being fun and non-stressful. In the following example, Amy had been conditioned through her childhood experiences to associate meals with stress.

Pete was a stocky union organizer and precinct committeeman who was disturbed by his wife's eating disorder. "She eats like a bird," Pete complained. "I try to get her to sit down and relax at the table with the family, but she stands in front of the sink with her shoulders hunched up and eats a few bites off her plate. If anything stressful is going on, she stops eating altogether."

Throughout her childhood, dinner had been a stressful event for Amy. "Everyone sat at the table noticing that Dad wasn't there. We all had our secret thoughts, but we pretended nothing was wrong. Sometimes he was drunk in another room in the house, unable to come to the table, and still we would act as though nothing was amiss. The few times he made it to the table reasonably sober no one knew how to act. We did not know what to say to one another. There was no small talk." On a few occasions neither parent was home for dinner, and Amy's older brother took the two younger children next door and told the neighbors they were hungry. The neighbors fed them peanut butter and jelly sandwiches. The children begged the neighbors not to say anything to their parents when they returned home. Even though Amy said her parents never fought (children of alcoholics often emphasize that there was no violence), there was always an underlying tension between the parents and within the family. Amy said that her stomach would tighten up and hurt during those times and she would be unable to eat.

Pete listened to Amy's memories of her childhood meals with her family. They discussed what they might do together to reduce Amy's mealtime tension now that she was a mother with her own family. They decided to make their mealtimes as consistent, predictable, and stress-free as possible. They joined a church as a family and practiced their faith together. They set dinnertime for six o'clock each evening and began with the family holding hands at the table and offering thanks. Holding each other's hands reminded them of their love for one another and God's love for them, and acknowledging their many blessings and the food they were about to receive reminded them how fortunate they were. As Pete said, "It is all downhill after you count your blessings."

Pete and Amy encouraged their children to share their day's experiences at the table. Amy, Pete, and the kids decided upon a schedule of meals. The children enjoyed the predictability of the menus, as well as coming home from school to the delicious aroma of a home-cooked meal. Amy enjoyed preparing the evening meal and found that cooking was one way she could show the family how much she loved them. The structured mealtime became more comfortable for all of them. The role of the calm, loving mother sitting down at the table with the family was a new one for Amy. At first she felt phony trying to act as though she was June Cleaver, but, in time, she became comfortable with her motherly role. Dinner with the family became a pleasant experience instead of an ordeal.

In this example of tension expressing itself as an eating disorder, Pete did several helpful things for Amy and for the relationship. He allowed her to describe the stresses she associated with meals during her childhood and he empathized with her childhood experiences, understanding that her current symptoms were products of her childhood trauma. The two of them developed a plan to reduce the stresses she associated with family meals. Amy was not cured, but she was much better. She could enjoy meals with her family. Under stressful conditions her old fears and tension would sometimes emerge, but she was able to discuss the situation with Pete and nearly always find a way to relax.

Insomnia is another malady that frequently results from the childhood conditioning experienced by many adult children. Some people jump into bed and pull the covers over their heads in an effort to shut out the world, while others find it impossible to sleep. Maggie belonged to the latter group and sought help for insomnia. She came to our office accompanied by her husband, Bill. He appeared worn out, with a rumpled appearance reminiscent of Detective Columbo. Bill's first question was whether there might be a sedative Maggie could take to get some sleep. Maggie offered that throughout her childhood her alcoholic father had worked on a dangerous job as a city policeman on the night shift. When there were emergencies, he was called back to duty after he had started drinking. Maggie said on those nights, "I stayed awake crying and biting my fingernails, worrying that dad might be shot or accidentally shoot someone else. When Dad wasn't working he stayed out late at the bars and I worried he might be killed in an auto accident—because he had been in accidents while drinking. When he came home at night my parents would argue. I stayed up in my room, listening and hoping they wouldn't fight and, when they did, I worried that mom might get hurt."

Bill permitted Maggie to relate her childhood experiences in detail. He told her, "I am sorry you had such a stressful time growing up. You know that I do not drink and I do not stay out late. On the rare occasions when I do have to be away, I will call you and let you know that I am okay."

Maggie employed some sleep hygiene techniques in her effort to relax and sleep at night. She exercised earlier in the day, and she followed a sleep ritual in which she went to bed at the same time each night and followed the same schedule of undressing, having a warm glass of milk, brushing her teeth, taking a warm bath, and turning out the lights. She used the bedroom only for sleeping; she did not watch television or read there. She also used some progressive relaxation techniques and deep-breathing exercises to help herself relax.

Bill continued to reassure her of his support and that they were both okay. Bill encouraged Maggie to take life one day at a time and not to worry about things that haven't happened yet or that didn't happen in the past. "Does a tree in the forest worry about forest fires?" he asked her. "'What ifs' are in the future and 'If onlys' are in the past. All we have is the 'now' and we should be grateful and make the most of it," Bill told her. On some occasions, however, Bill encouraged Maggie to continue to talk about the things she felt she missed growing up and her feelings about them. As a helpful exercise, Maggie wrote a letter to her father describing in detail what she'd missed throughout her childhood because of his drinking. Then she tore up the letter. The exercise helped her recall other childhood feelings that she shared with Bill.

Maggie found that within a few months she was able to experience restful sleep on most nights. She said that the most important factor in her improvement was talking about her feelings as a child and Bill's understanding and support. It was not important that he offer solutions, but it was important that he understood what she was saying and that he validated her feelings. They both realized that this was a lengthy process of recognizing the things that were missing in her childhood, acknowledging her feelings about the lack of nurturing while growing up, and eventually accepting that she could not go back and correct what she missed. Bill even surprised her with a hot tub as a present; they both said it helped them relax and sleep.

By encouraging Maggie to talk about the problem and listening empathetically and without passing judgment, Bill understood why she was having trouble sleeping as an adult. At times, he encouraged her to try to recall the details of her childhood experiences and to share them and her feelings with him. Although the expression of chronic tension can vary, partners can help adult children reduce their stress by empathizing, encouraging discussion about their experiences, validating their feelings, and providing a consistent predictable environment. Over time, such efforts may help their partner to recognize and mourn the ambiguous losses they sustained as children and, as a result, enjoy freedom from chronic tension.

HE HAD A HAT

DOOM AND GLOOM FROM WOMB TO TOMB

Henny Youngman used to tell a story about a Jewish grandmother who took her grandson to Miami Beach. The boy went into the ocean and was swept out to sea by the undertow. The lifeguards went after him in boats and helicopters. They pulled him from the sea, put him on the beach, and gave him CPR. The boy coughed up some seawater and was saved. The lifeguards looked up at the grandmother, who merely responded, "He had a hat." In this chapter we will talk about the tendency for adult children to anticipate negative outcomes and to maintain a pessimistic attitude.

UNDERLYING FACTORS RESPONSIBLE FOR CHRONIC DYSPHORIA (PAINFUL FEELING, MILD DEPRESSION)

In psychiatry, when we find ourselves treating a patient for depression who is not responding, we ask ourselves, "Is there an underlying medical problem we have missed? Is there a chemical-dependency problem the patient has kept hidden from us? Or, are there traumatic experiences the patient has repressed?" Many adult children of alcoholics experience a chronic, smoldering mild depression (dysthymia) because they have repressed the painful childhood experiences and significant losses they sustained growing up. There are basically three psychological causes for their sadness and pessimistic outlook on life: (1) On the surface, it is a psychological defense adult children developed to lessen the pain of disappointment they felt as children. (2) At a deeper level, it reflects the sadness they experienced, and still experience, due to the ambiguous loss of an emotional relationship with their parents. Pauline Boss, author of *Ambiguous Loss: Learning to Live with Unresolved Grief*, refers to this as "frozen grief." (3) It is an accompanying false guilt that comes from their remorse for their parent's behavior ("false" as opposed to the guilt that comes from one's own wrongdoing). Children are egocentric and feel that whatever happens around them has to do with them. When parents die the children think that they passed away because the children were not good enough or the parents did not find them lovable enough to want to stay with them. In the case of an alcoholic parent, the child feels somehow responsible for the parent's drinking and feels like a failure because she or he was unable to get the parent to stop drinking. When these children become adults they do not think that way consciously, but the guilt and self-recrimination remains. In psychotherapy adult children become aware of their irrational guilt feelings as children that stemmed from their shame for failing to stop their parent from drinking.

PESSIMISM AS A DEFENSE AGAINST DISAPPOINTMENT

Children who grow up in alcoholic homes develop a negative weltanschauung (worldview) as a defense against the constant disappointment they experienced. Kelly said she would pray that her father would not drink, but he always did. When she got older she'd find his cache of liquor and pour it out. Kelly substituted water for the vodka in the bottles and hoped that this would lessen his intoxication. Her father discovered the watered-down vodka, however, and went into a rage that terrified her. He promised he would take her to the zoo but got drunk and forgot; he said he'd be at her piano concert but went to the bars instead. "After a while, no matter what he promised, I told myself it isn't going to happen and it usually did not. I told myself that things are going to be bad—and they usually were. It didn't hurt quite as much as when I had my hopes up." If you ask your adult child about her or his childhood experience, your partner will tell you that it was not all bad. In some ways it might have been less stressful for them had it been all bad—at least it would have been predictable. Remember the experiment with the rat on the grid? The rat developed stress symptoms when it was randomly shocked and had no control of the situation. The same was true for your partner. Once in a while the alcoholic parent would keep a promise, and occasionally things did turn out okay. It is this inconsistency that made things so out of control and stressful for your companion.

Betty Ann's mother divorced Betty Ann's alcoholic father when he became involved in illegal behavior, became physically abusive, and she could no longer deny his infidelity. Later, when her mother remarried, Betty Ann's stepfather legally adopted her. Betty Ann reported that her biological father would call her while intoxicated and tell her, "You are a terrible daughter. No one will ever want you. You will never get married." On other occasions he would remind her that she was his daughter and was just like him. Betty Ann said she knew that he was drunk and was angry because she no longer acknowledged him as her father, but his statements hurt her and caused her to feel that she was defective. "I kept thinking that half of my genes were from him and maybe I was half evil. Whenever I dated anyone I would think that it would only be a matter of time before they found out how bad I was and leave me." Unfortunately, Betty Ann's experience is shared to some degree by many adult children. In many alcoholic families, criticism and guilt-producing condemnation were present. Many non-recovering alcoholics blame the people closest to them for their illness. "If you would quit nagging, I would not have to drink. If these kids would shut up. If I did not have to pay these bills. So what if I drink too much—you spend too much." This sometimes becomes circular logic in which the alcoholic says, "My wife does not understand me." The bartender asks,

"Why doesn't she understand you?" "Because I drink." "Why do you drink?" asks the bartender. "Because my wife does not understand me." This addiction-based logic and blaming played a role in your partner's negative self-image.

Adult children of alcoholics have learned to expect negative outcomes since as children they learned that optimism led to greater pain and disappointment. They carry this negative outlook into adult life and tend to see the glass as half empty. Scott, a middle-aged accountant and adult child, told us, "I have ocular rectitis. My optic nerve is connected to my rectum, which gives me a crappy outlook on life." Another adult child said his motto was "Every cloud has a crappy lining." Sue said, "I'm a WCS (worst-case scenario) person." Alcoholics Anonymous has a saying: "Fear is the darkroom where negatives are developed."

VICTIMIZATION

Your adult child was a victim growing up. Your partner probably blamed him- or herself for the problems in the family and felt undeserving of love and attention, but the fact is that your partner was an innocent child who grew up with parents who had serious problems and who were unable to give their children the unconditional love and security they needed. As we have seen, ACOAs are often attracted to relationships that mimic the ones they had with their alcoholic parent. Again, they find themselves to be victims. As adults they are voluntary victims, meaning they have the ability to set boundaries to protect themselves or leave an unhealthy relationship but often don't. Your companion realized that he or she has been attracted to unhealthy relationships in the past and has selected you as a potentially healthy partner. It takes time for ACOAs to become accustomed to a relationship with a caring individual. In the meantime, your partner may misperceive events in a way that supports an unconscious expectation that you will disappoint and hurt him or her.

Melanie was a thirty-two-year-old medical office manager who had been through several abusive relationships before coming to the realization that she was consistently picking men who did not respect her boundaries. She made a conscious effort to find a man who was gentle and respectful. Brian was a minister who was single. They were married after an extended period of dating and engagement. Melanie began to feel that Brian was more attached to his church and his parishioners than he was to her. She resented being in the limelight and having to meet the approval of the congregation. She started obsessing: "Why do I have to please everyone? Why do my needs always have to be last? Why do I have to stay home while Brian goes to church conferences?" Melanie remembered that she'd obsessed in the same way when she was in the abusive relationships in the past. Brian reminded her that he'd explained his job as a pastor and her role as a minister's wife before they were married. "God is first in my life, but you are second," he said. "The meetings are part of the job. You are in a fishbowl, but you are a wonderful person and everyone in the church can see that." "My relationship with Brian was nothing like my relationship with my dad or the abusive relationships I had experienced in the past, but I was unconsciously trying to make myself feel that it was." Melanie asked Brian to remind her of this whenever she began obsessing or picturing herself as a victim.

ACCENTUATE THE POSITIVE

If you recognize that your partner has a tendency to be negative, have her or him tell you about childhood experiences and how that negative outlook protected her or him from greater disappointment and pain. Point out that your companion and her or his current environment are different now and that as an adult, your ACOA does not have to put up with anyone who does not keep his or her word. Encourage a positive outlook. Emphasize the positive aspects of your companion's childhood and the positive events in her or his present life. As the Alcoholics Anonymous slogan goes, "Develop an attitude of gratitude." Note that your partnership is the start of a loving family. The Chinese say that the mind is a flexible container that molds itself to whatever you put in it. That is, if a person reads tragedies they are going to become sad, and if they read comedies they will feel happy. Therefore, suggest that your partner take in positive messages—through reading, listening to recordings, and watching videos—so she or he can shift thoughts in a more positive direction. Many adult children find it helpful to read and listen to positive affirmations each day. By doing so they are attempting to reprogram the negative tapes in their heads that they received from their early interactions with their parents. Everyone is susceptible to negative influences in daily interactions. As a psychiatrist was leaving his dermatologist's office, the skin doctor said, "Stay out of the sun." The psychiatrist turned and asked him, "Why? Do I have a problem that requires me to stay out of the sun?" "No," the dermatologist answered. "I say that to all my patients. Don't you shrinks have any general advice you give to all of your patients?" The psychiatrist thought a moment and then answered, "Well, let's see. Don't watch the news."

The ancient Greeks thought that depression was caused by an excess of black bile in the system, so they called the condition melan (black) cholia (bile), or melancholy. The Greek treatment for melancholy was to have depressed patients watch comedies and listen to music. (They also had them use laxatives—which did not turn out to be that helpful.) Cognitive therapists attempt to have their depressed patients turn their negative thoughts into positive ones. You can review each day the many blessings you and your partner have received, and when you pray together at dinner, thank God for all you have been given.

Sports psychologists have learned that whenever a person is emotional, that particular experience tends to be retained in their muscle memory. As a result they advise golfers to become emotional about the good shots but to remain calm and objective about the bad ones (most of us do just the opposite). This is good advice for life. Get excited about the positive events and forget those that are not so good.

Al was a good-natured insurance agent who was married to Sally, a real-estate salesperson who was also an adult child. Sally tended to be pessimistic. Al said that he'd heard Bishop Sheen tell a story about a pessimistic barber. No matter what anyone told him, he would turn it into a negative situation. A customer came into the shop and announced that he'd won a contest and was getting a free trip to Rome, Italy. "Yeah," said the barber. "What airline are you going to fly on?"

"I do not know," answered the customer. The barber replied, "I'll tell you, it will probably be some Italian airline, you will be packed in like sardines, and you will be lucky if you make it. Where are you going to stay when you get there?" "I don't know," answered the customer. "It will be some firetrap, probably filled with rats and cockroaches, with a bathroom down the hall," said the barber, shaking his head, "and what are you supposed to do when you get there?" "I am supposed to have a private audience with the pope," the customer replied. "Oh yeah, it will be you and thousands of screaming Italians—that will be your private audience," said the barber. The customer left and returned a few weeks later. "How was your trip?" asked the barber. "Great," answered the customer. "I flew American Airlines first class to Rome, stayed in a suite in a five-star hotel, and had a private audience with the pope." "A private audience with the pope!" whispered the incredulous barber. "What did he say to you?" "Well, when I bent over to kiss his ring he asked, 'Where did you get that lousy haircut?'"

ATTITUDE THERAPY

Victor Frankel was a Jewish psychoanalyst who was sent to a Nazi concentration camp during World War II. He witnessed his family's executions. Frankel decided that he was not going to get depressed and told himself, "They can torture me and kill me—but they can't control my attitude." In the words of Schiller's William Tell, "Die Gedanken Sind Frei" (The thoughts are free). Frankel started smiling and doing nice things for other prisoners. The other prisoners, who were depressed and preoccupied with the miserable conditions of the camp, cheered up in response to his positive attitude. The guards felt guilty when they saw Frankel's compassion for his fellow prisoners. His positive attitude and caring nature confronted them with their own inhumanity. Encouraged by the changes Frankel felt in himself and saw in those around him as the result of his positive attitude, he published a book on "attitude therapy" after his liberation. Frankel said, "It is what you are thinking rather than the situation that prompts you to feel and act the way you do. Nothing outside of you can make you feel or act in any particular way." Few people would have Frankel's ability to maintain a positive attitude in the conditions of a concentration camp, but we can use his example as an inspiration to develop a positive attitude in our present circumstances.

Adult children often have punitive consciences. They frequently beat themselves up over what their superegos tell them they *ought–should–could* be doing. Whenever you hear your companion using those words, you know that their consciences are giving them a hard time. Your partner developed a pessimistic outlook in part as a defense against disappointment during childhood. Encourage her or him to take the risk of being optimistic and hopeful as an adult. Abraham Lincoln said, "Most folks are about as happy as they make up their minds to be." Alcoholics Anonymous says, "Life is a millstone—*you* decide if it is going to grind you down or polish you up." Some ACOAs write down their self-critical thoughts and put the notes in a box they refer to as their "God Box." They are turning these critical thoughts over to God and freeing themselves to go let go of the self-criticism. Others find it helpful to write their own positive affirmations by using the technique recommended by cognitive therapists and turning their negative thoughts into positive ones. For example, the thought "I am so dumb," can be changed to "I am pretty clever; I figured out the source of my negative thoughts." "I cannot do anything right" can be changed by thinking "That is what my alcoholic father used to tell me as a kid. I know now that he was projecting his own feelings of inadequacy onto me. I realize, as an adult, that I do many things correctly in my life and the criticism I received as a child was not warranted and was, in fact, Dad's problem." Continually changing negative thoughts into positive ones has the effect of dampening the harsh, critical parent that is present in one's conscience and replacing that negative image with positive, encouraging messages.

DYSPHORIA AS A RESULT OF CHILDHOOD LOSSES THAT CANNOT BE REPLACED

In addition to telling your partner jokes, helping your partner count his or her blessings, and encouraging your partner to change negative messages into positive ones, you can help this individual take one day at a time. The past is gone, the future is not here yet, and today is all we have, so we might as well make the best of it. Once your adult child feels secure in his or her present life with you, he or she can then review childhood experiences from the perspective of a safe, loving relationship in the present. Your adult child can see that his or her folks did the best they could. Alcoholism is an illness and it affects the whole family. As children ACOAs listened to their parents and tried to make sense from what they heard. As adults they can now see that much of the thinking was irrational and the product of the parents' problems. They can see that they were good kids who were trying to adapt to an abnormal environment, and they can readjust their distorted self-images in the light of their present-day relationships.

As we have mentioned previously, the behavioral patterns exhibited by adult children need to be recognized and addressed by caregivers when medications are prescribed. If they are not, ACOAs will likely become anxious and think they are experiencing a "reaction" to the medicine that is actually their anxiety about losing control and their anticipation of a negative outcome. Sometimes adult children are diagnosed as having a depressive illness. In many cases, they aren't clinically depressed—they are chronically dysphoric and suffering from "frozen grief" because of the unresolved ambiguous losses they sustained in childhood. Bradshaw feels this chronic depressive state is the result of toxic shame that causes the individual to believe that she or he is defective as a human being. Antidepressant medication isn't the answer for this problem. The correct approach is for the patient to recognize the childhood losses, accept that things will never be the way she or he wished in childhood, and mourn the absence of a different emotional relationship with her or his parents. To help adult children recapture childhood feelings, we have them perform an exercise in which they write letters to their addicted parent and address all the things they missed during childhood because of their parent's alcoholic disease. Then we have them tear up the letters. This task is designed to help the ACOAs recall more events and feelings from their childhood—not to try to educate their alcoholic parent.

One of our patients, Dawn, wrote a detailed letter, but instead of destroying it, she called her nonrecovering father and read her letter to him over the phone. His response was, "Well, it's real good to hear from you, and we'll have to have more of these talks again real soon." Dawn was devastated. She felt worse than before because her father did not understand anything she said to him and never would. Although this was an upsetting experience, Dawn later realized it was at this point that she finally accepted the fact that she was never going to have the father she wanted, nor was there any hope for them to have a real emotional relationship. He was controlled by his illness. Unfortunately, as in many alcoholic homes, Dawn's mother was codependent and preoccupied with the father's disease. Her mother was drained and was unable to give much love or support to her children. Dawn said, "What little love was available was conditional. Both of our parents received gratification from my brother's football and my cheerleading. We knew our performance was important to them." Dawn came to the conclusion that she had to mourn the absence of an emotional relationship with both of her parents.

Jenny married an abusive workaholic, who she later recognized as being similar to her violent, alcoholic father. After one episode, in which her husband choked and beat her in front of her children, she called her mother in tears to tell her what had happened. Her mother responded, "We are in the process of moving to Tucson, Arizona." "But mother," she sobbed. "My husband just beat me—my eyes are blackened. I don't know what to do." Ignoring Jenny's distress, the mother continued, "We had to move. The people who lived upstairs were terrible." Jenny realized that her mother would never be available to her for understanding or support.

Adult children may neglect themselves and their own health. Sensitive to the needs of others, they have difficulty taking time for themselves. There is an old saying: "If you do not take time to be well, you will take time to be sick." By encouraging your partner to eat healthy foods, take time out to exercise, and get regular checkups from the doctor, you will also be helping his or her morale. Exercise can become a healthy addiction. It relieves tension, reduces weight, sustains health, and can have an antidepressant effect. The Chinese admonish, "He who eats less eats more," meaning if you eat less you live longer and end up eating more.

In conclusion, you can help your partner dispel dysphoria and pessimism by encouraging her or him to emphasize the positive, count her or his blessings, read affirmations, pray, avoid the news, consciously try to maintain an optimistic attitude, and try to turn negative thoughts into positive ones. Help your partner establish a secure life in the present. Then, from the perspective of your safe, loving relationship, encourage your loved one to identify and mourn the loss of an emotional relationship with her or his parents. An Alcoholics Anonymous saying is "Look at your past, but do not stare at it." In other words, it is appropriate to know how your adult behavioral patterns were created and how your thoughts and feelings as a child were different than they are now as an adult—but do not dwell on past trauma. Also, do not use the trauma of childhood as an excuse for your adult difficulties. As they say in Alcoholics Anonymous, "Get off the cross—we need the wood."

THEY DON'T KNOW
THEY'RE BEAUTIFUL

B ert and Carolyn were journalists who had been married for over
ten years. Carolyn was an ACOA who had gone the usual route
of having a few bad relationships and then realizing that she had unconsciously chosen these unreliable men on the basis of her childhood
patterns. She read about adult children and had considerable insight
into her childhood patterns by the time she dated Bert. Her ability to
introspect caused Bert to think of his own childhood and the two of
them discussed how his early experiences had influenced his adult reactions. Their relationship became progressively more intimate over the
years. They coauthored their first book together, and the publisher re-
quested that they have a photograph taken for the book jacket. Bert
described the experience.

> Carolyn was dragging her feet about scheduling the picture and
> seemed to be coming up with one reason or another why she could
> not have it taken. This was not unusual as she tends to procrastinate,
> and so I went ahead and set the date for the photographer to come

to the house. Carolyn got her hair and nails done and went shopping for a new outfit to wear in the picture. She told her mother and her best friend that she was fat, but she did not care how she looked in the picture; they would just have to take her as she was. The night before the photographer was to arrive, we were watching television together when I got a long-distance phone call from my brother. As I was trying to hear on the phone, Carolyn deliberately turned up the volume on the television. I had to leave the room to complete the call. I mentioned that I thought this was rather rude on her part, and she went ballistic. She started screaming that she always left the room when she got a call and that if I was angry with her, she was going to leave the house. And, she added, "I am not having my picture taken tomorrow." I finally got her calmed down enough to stay with the agreement that we would sleep in separate bedrooms. The following day she got ready for the photograph but told me, "You owe me big time." The actual photograph took about ten minutes and was relatively painless. When the proofs of the pictures were finished, Carolyn looked great as she always does. I showed them to her and she said, "They are okay," which was the best she could say about her photographic image.

When we later discussed the incident, Carolyn said she had been worrying about having her picture taken for two weeks. She said she was fat, she looked old, her hair was not right, and she always looked terrible in pictures. I thought I was over being surprised by Carolyn's reactions to things, but I could not believe what she was saying. Carolyn is extremely attractive and photogenic. She always looks great in pictures. I told her this, but she thought I was just trying to pacify her. She admitted that she probably picked a fight and overreacted the night before in an effort to get out of having her picture taken. She told me how, when she was twelve, she'd had another girl throw a softball at her in order to deliberately injure her fingers so that she could get out of a piano recital she had been dreading. She said that this scenario reminded her of that experience.

Your adult child is most likely a talented, hardworking, loyal person who underestimates his or her abilities and, as in Carolyn's case, appearance. Focusing on the common adult-child behavioral patterns that may affect your relationship might cause you to think that your partner has a great many problems. This is not the case. Adult children are humble and feel that they are different from other adults; they tend to stay on the periphery of social situations; and they will let their partner take the lead in the relationship, assuming that the other individual is "healthier" and "more normal." Most adult children have great potential. In many cases their insecurities and lack of self-confidence have inhibited the expression of their talents. Ideally, your relationship will help your adult child grow in confidence, nurture his or her many skills, and permit your adult child to share those talents with the world at large.

ACOAs frequently appear to be self-confident individuals. Although they often feel insecure in social situations, they publicly present themselves as articulate and self-assured. They are hardworking, easy to please, and are loyal to the organization. Employers like them because they tend to avoid confrontation and don't usually ask for raises. This is part of the façade of normalcy and adequacy they have presented to the world since childhood, having learned early in life to put on a front and act like everything was okay at home. Frequently, the love they received was conditional and based on their success in the community. ACOAs were often the scholars, the jocks, and the popular students. They attempted to please their parents and to compensate for their family's as well as their own shame and embarrassment. Adult children were sensitive to the feelings of others and "people pleasers," which almost always leads to being well liked and popular in school. Inwardly, they felt different, inadequate, unattractive, and ashamed of their home situation. They experienced the toxic shame described by John Bradshaw and tried to act like the other kids who had "normal" families.

Children need and like discipline. When it is inconsistent or non-existent, they may set their own rules, pretending the parents are setting the guidelines. One adult child, Marge, said that her mother was drunk most of the time and that she had a series of "dads" who had little or no interest in her. She had no role models and no rules at home. She joined a church youth group and tried to imitate the other girls there. When a boy would take her to a dance, she would say that she had to be in by ten o'clock because she heard her girlfriends say this. "Actually, my mother would not have known if I had been gone for a week," Marge later commented. She credited her youth group as being the source of her stability during her adolescent years. Marge later went on to do well in college and had a happy, stable adult life and a good marriage. She continued to be a member of the church that had supported her as a youngster and kept her on the right path in life.

As mentioned earlier, children are naturally self-centered and, as a result, assume that they are the cause of the events around them. As children, ACOAs felt responsible for their alcoholic parent's drinking and guilty that they could not make that parent stop. Their parents were wrapped up with the disease of alcoholism and did not provide the attention, unconditional love, security, and identity models the children needed, but these kids assumed they did not receive these necessities because something was wrong with them: they were not worthy of love.

Initially it may seem that your good-looking partner is being humble and modest about his or her appearance, but as you get better acquainted, you realize your partner really does not see him or herself as attractive or lovable. When compliments are given for your companion's appearance or for their many talents and strengths, he or she may have difficulty accepting the praise. It is important for you to continue to give positive feedback, no matter what the response. However, just telling your adult child that he or she is good-looking and talented isn't going to solve the problem. As we mentioned previously, sharing your own childhood experiences and letting your partner help you with your adult patterns of behavior demonstrates your need to depend on your companion just as much as they need to lean on you. Letting your adult child help you allows him or her to feel valuable and needed, thus reinforcing what you've been trying to share about his or her talents and skills.

Kids who grow up in homes where their parents thank God everyday for sending them this wonderful child grow up with tremendous self-confidence and self-esteem. They walk into a room and think, "These people are thrilled to have me in their presence," and people tend to respond to them in a positive way. Kids who grow up in an alcoholic home grow up being criticized and blamed for the parent's shortcomings, feeling guilty, having little self-worth, and feeling they do not have any control or choice about events in their lives. You can do a great deal to boost both the self-confidence and self-esteem of your adult child by loving her or him unconditionally and without judgment. When someone knows everything about you and still loves you, it makes you feel good about yourself.

You can also boost your adult child's self-esteem and self-confidence by not getting in the way of her or his growth and development as an adult. Encourage and support your ACOA's goals and aspirations and help her or him to realize that she or he has choices in life. In a truly loving relationship, each person is free to develop as an individual. Your humble adult child will tend to support you and stay in the background, but you can encourage your partner to think about her or his many talents and how to use and express them in life. Janet, Carol, and Angela are extreme examples of individuals who successfully overcame severe childhood trauma with its accompanying low self-esteem and low self-confidence.

Janet was a woman in her fifties whose parents were both alcoholics. When Janet was a child, her dad beat her, and her mother once threatened to kill her with a knife. As an adult she dated an abusive alcoholic and married him on the spur of the moment. Janet lived with him for over twenty-five years, during which time he beat her and was unfaithful to her. When she had a miscarriage, her mother told her she was too old to have children anyway. Janet became addicted and while on a chemical-dependency unit, participated in an exercise with her husband to inspire trust. He was to catch her when she let herself fall backward. Instead, he jumped aside, let her fall, and then laughed at her. Janet finally divorced him when she discovered he had another family and was living a double life. She met Brad, an insurance company claims adjustor who had experienced a difficult marriage and divorce. This was the first time in her life that she was able to have a trusting relationship. She said she enjoyed sex with him and was able, for the first time, to experience an orgasm. She began to think more of herself, and as a result, she looked and functioned better than she had in previous years. She felt more confident in herself and more secure in general. As she felt better about herself, she noticed that people responded to her at work in a more positive manner. As she recovered, her main worry was that something would happen to Brad.

Carol grew up in an urban ghetto. Her parents were both addicted to alcohol and drugs. Her father was mentally and physically abusive to her mother and to the children. The Department of Children and Family Services removed Carol from her alcoholic parents when neighbors heard her screaming, and she was discovered neglected in her crib, being eaten by rats. She was placed in a foster home and was fortunate to have foster parents who were loving and supportive. The effects of the trauma she sustained with her birth parents remained despite her change in environment. As a child Carol excelled in school and she was always neat and clean and well dressed. She said she never wanted anyone to be able to guess what she had been through as a child. She looked like a fashion model and had no trouble getting dates. Her initial relationships turned out to be with abusive, self-centered men who tended to be dependent and critical. Later, Carol was able to reflect on her unhappy relationships and saw she was repeating the abuse she sustained as a child. She consciously chose a kind, dependable magazine editor named Maurice. She said she would have overlooked him in her younger years as being "boring." Early in their relationship, Carol would periodically accuse Maurice of hurting her, disappointing her, lying to her, and being selfish. He remained calm during her tirades and expressed his confusion about her behavior. Carol was able to distance herself from her feelings and observe that she was relating to her gentle husband as if he were her abusive father or one of the abusive men she had known in the past. She was able to share the reasons for her explosive anger and false accusations with Maurice, who listened to her and could understand the connection between her childhood trauma and her outbursts toward him. Maurice remained calm and loyal, and she knew that he loved her as a person. She came to realize she had many strengths and attributes, that her father's criticism was unjustified, and that she was loved and safe in her adult life. As Carol began to make healthy choices, she began to have more confidence in herself and more energy to devote to constructive activities. Carol obtained a PhD in psychology and wrote several successful books.

At the time Angela was born, her alcoholic dad was in bed with his mistress. She said that her father was "the life of the party" and much more fun than her mother, but he was seldom home. He maintained his relationship with his mistress until he died. Angela said she loved and admired her dad, but he was rarely available to her. Her mother was sullen and critical of her. There was no physical violence but constant tension and frequent arguments when the parents were together. Angela's main coping device was trying to please others. With reflection, she understood it was a way to control others. She would do for others with the expectation that they would respond by doing as she wished. Angela said that her self-esteem was so low that she felt no one could love her, and she felt the only value she had for others was what she could do for them. She said she finally learned that "if I do not want to be a doormat, I need to get up off the floor." Angela made a conscious effort to look for nonaddicted men and, as a result, met her husband, Paul. He reported that early in their marriage Angela continually checked with her friends and relatives before making a final decision. He said she had to validate her thoughts and feelings because she was so insecure about herself. When Angela shopped she always went with another woman who could help her "choose the right things." Paul said Angela lacked confidence in her ability to select her own wardrobe, was insecure about decorating their house, and questioned her landscaping choices as well. Paul told her that she had excellent taste in all aspects of their life, and he encouraged her to go with her gut feelings and select and arrange things the way she thought they should be. He told her that if she walked in to a room with fifty people, she would have fifty different opinions and she couldn't control any of them. He praised her appearance and complimented her on her decorating and gardening. Their friends and relatives also chimed in with compliments. Angela said that, in time, she developed confidence in her abilities and tastes and became less dependent on the opinions of others. Paul would frequently tell Angela that he loved her just as she was and that while he supported her growth in any way that brought her happiness, she didn't have to do anything or prove anything to win his affection. Angela gave Paul credit for her increased self-confidence. Angela said, "Paul's constant admiration and assurance helped me feel that I was competent and able to make good choices. At first, I found it difficult to accept the fact that his love was unconditional, but, in time, I could see that it was. Paul knows everything about me and still loves me."

Love is not a one-way street. Your "job" in your relationship is not to love your ACOA unconditionally and "cure" them. You have your own patterns and your adult child knows you well. The fact that he or she knows you so completely and still loves you unconditionally will help you make positive changes in yourself. For example, Chad said that he was overcontrolled and inhibited most of his life. He couldn't believe that his wife, Heather, an adult child, was attracted to him. Heather was energetic and exciting. She surprised and shocked Chad with her passion and impulsiveness. As their relationship progressed Chad said that Heather's love helped him change. She convinced him to take dancing lessons with her. Prior to their marriage, he had been phobic about dancing and would perspire and hyperventilate at the thought of getting out on the dance floor. Because Chad knew Heather enjoyed dancing, he took the lessons and, to his surprise, found that it was enjoyable. Chad said that he felt that he had been "in jail" most of his life and that Heather had helped him break out of his inhibited, phobic lifestyle. He said he identified with Jack Nicholson's character in *As Good As It Gets*, feeling that Heather's love had cured most of his obsessive-compulsive symptoms

In many good relationships there is attraction based on admiration of traits in the other person that you feel are lacking in yourself. "Opposites attract" has some truth to it. The difference between couples who grow closer and those who grow apart is the extent to which the individuals are able to learn from each other. Jennifer was an adult child who was anxious in social situations and mistrusting of others, but very well organized, a good planner, and able to budget her money. She was in a relationship with Tom, who was comfortable socially. Everyone liked him immediately because he was so open and genuine. Under stress Jennifer would become intense and attempt to "fix" whatever was bothering Tom. Tom would retreat and attempt to avoid closeness and discussion. This caused tension between them. As they discussed their situation, Tom acknowledged that Jennifer had good intentions and wanted to help him, while he wanted his "space" to attempt to deal with his problems. Jennifer said she could accept this but wanted to know what was worrying him because she interpreted his withdrawal as his reacting negatively to something she had done. As they discussed their relationship, Tom said he felt he could benefit from Jennifer's ability to organize, plan, and budget, and Jennifer said she felt she could try to emulate Tom's openness and positive attitude. As a result they grew closer as a couple and benefited from their partner's attributes.

Tammy said that, in time, she knew that her husband, Leo, loved her, and this helped her overcome her low self-esteem and self-confidence. "Whenever I would start beating myself up, I would think, 'Leo loves me, so I must be good in some ways.'" She said later she was able to think more positively about herself without needing Leo's reassurance. Leo, who was an adult child, said that it worked both ways. "Tammy tells me things I need to do to improve. I do not see it as criticism or a put-down. I know she loves me and she is telling me these things for my own good. So I try to listen to what she is saying and do what she suggests."

Loving your partner and being loved by them is a great source of strength and a boost to both of your self-esteems. A loving relationship makes you both stronger because you each have a safe, trusted friend who will validate your feelings and will also tell you things about yourself that no one else can or will. Even better, because you love and trust your partner, you will listen to what he or she has to say. You will help your companion realize that he or she has choices in life and that you will support your companion's efforts to grow and to develop his or her skills and talents. Validate your ACOA's feelings, praise his or her successes, and minimize his or her mistakes. To err is human; it's better to make a mistake than not to try new things. A group of us visited our friend, a prominent lawyer who was on his deathbed. His last words to us were, "If there is anything you have been thinking about doing in life—do it now, because you do not know what will happen tomorrow."

MOUNTAINS FROM MOLEHILLS

C hildren in alcoholic homes experienced periodic crises due to their parent's drinking: Dad comes home drunk and the parents fight. Dad does not come home and is involved in an accident. Dad gives away the family dog. Both parents are unfaithful. Dad breaks down the front door of the house with an ax. Dad rapes the babysitter while Mom is in the hospital having a baby. Mom gets drunk and nearly drowns in the pool. Mom throws the dinner against the wall and the children have to clean it up. Dad loses his job because of drinking. Mom falls asleep and sets the house on fire. Dad and Mom divorce. Dad tries to break into the house, and Mom kills him. These are actual events described by adult children of alcoholics over the years.

Most of us walk around in a state of denial. We do not think that the airplane or car we are riding in will crash. We do not think that we are going to be ill. We act as though we plan to live forever, and we are surprised when a relative or friend dies. We do not expect to be robbed or assaulted, and we are not worried that a tornado, flood, earthquake, blizzard, or other natural disaster is going to adversely affect our lives.

Once something bad happens, it is difficult to maintain our denial of that event. For example, Steven, a state policeman, stopped a car for a traffic violation. As he approached the car to give the driver a citation, the driver leaned out and shot him. After this event, Steven was unable to perform his duties as a policeman. He feared that he would misinterpret a future driver's intent and shoot him or her, or that he would be too afraid to approach the next car he stopped.

Your adult child was exposed to many traumatic events during their childhood years; she or he knows that bad things do happen in life. In your partner's chaotic childhood experiences, the one predictable thing was that a crisis was going to occur. As a result of this, your adult child may perceive relatively minor stresses as major catastrophes or unconsciously create situations to produce crises in her or his life.

ADULT CHILDREN TEND TO ASSUME THE WORST

If you were called to your boss's office, you might assume that you were about to be rewarded for doing a good job. Adult children, however, are afraid of authority figures; they unconsciously remind adult children of their alcoholic parent. A call from their boss or a request to come to the boss's office ignites immediate anxiety as adult children anticipate that the boss is going to demote or fire them. For example, Samantha, an adult child, is a successful businesswoman who has a message on her answering machine requesting that the caller leave a detailed explanation of the reason for their call. She explained that if someone just leaves a phone number and she is unable to reach the caller immediately, she cannot sleep all night because she worries about the message and assumes it will be bad. Until proven otherwise, Samantha assumes anyone who calls has a negative message for her.

Adult children's negative preconceptions may produce selectivity in their hearing (what Bradshaw refers to as "filtering"). The boss may compliment them on their good work but make one suggestion, which is then taken as criticism. An extreme example of this type of selectivity was seen in Joseph, a middle-management worker in a large insurance company. Joseph's father had been an alcoholic. Joseph didn't drink but when he was driving his wife home from a nearby town late at night after a party, he fell asleep at the wheel and his wife was killed in the accident. Joseph was severely depressed and guilt-ridden. One of his fellow workers suggested that he might want to go to the library and read some books to distract himself. Joseph heard "lie" (from li-brary) and concluded that the fellow thought he was a liar. The point is, when you are thinking negative thoughts about yourself, you will tend to select or filter the statements of others to pick out those comments that support your own self-criticism.

Adult children often get into a "what-if" type of thinking that tends to dramatize and exaggerate the negative aspects of any situation. John was a white-collar worker who demonstrated the extreme of this phenomenon. He said that he had ruined his family financially, he was going to jail for embezzlement, and he might as well kill himself so that his family at least could collect on his life insurance. Later, when we were able to objectively evaluate John's job situation, we discovered that one of his tasks was to deposit the week's receipts in the bank on Friday after work. The previous Friday he had not gotten out of work until after the banks closed and had to make the deposit Saturday morning. As he began to fret about this, he reasoned, "I was twelve hours late making the deposit. This means that my employer was cheated out of twelve hours of interest on their money. Cheating is a form of embezzlement. Therefore, I am an embezzler. Embezzlers are criminals. Criminals go to prison. I will go to prison for my crime. My family will be without their breadwinner and will be destitute. The only thing I can do is take my life and let my family collect on my life insurance." In reviewing this situation with John, we were able to help him see that he hadn't committed a crime and that his boss wasn't upset with him about the twelve-hour delay in making the deposit.

This process is also referred to as "catastrophization," in which the person believes the worst possible outcome is the one most likely to happen. William, a computer analyst, started thinking he was drinking lots of fluid and urinating frequently. He did some reading and thought he might have diabetes. His family doctor examined him, obtained blood and urine tests for diabetes, and then reassured him that he absolutely did not have diabetes. William returned home and started feeling a tingling between his toes. He became anxious, didn't trust the doctor's reassurance, and started thinking, "That's diabetic peripheral neuropathy." His next thought was, "I will have to have insulin and I am so shaky—how will I be able to give myself a shot?"

PHYSICAL SYMPTOMS BECOME TERMINAL ILLNESSES

Adult children worry about illness. Any physical complaint may become exaggerated as they imagine the worst. They may misinterpret the doctor's expression and body language to confirm their negative suspicions. Nate worried about his vague physical complaints and ended up concluding that he had AIDS. He did not reveal his suspicions to his doctor but interpreted his doctor's facial expression and body language to mean that the doctor knew he had a terminal illness. Nate found it difficult to believe when his doctor told him he was in perfect health. Adult children assume the worst as they wait in fear for the results of their laboratory and X-ray tests. A test that is noted to be slightly abnormal or requires repeating is assumed to mean cancer.

Ruth was a twenty-six-year-old schoolteacher and an adult child. She was told that she had some cervical dysplasia, and her conservative gynecologist recommended a conization procedure as a precautionary measure. In Ruth's mind, her condition became cancer of the cervix. Two weeks later, she found a lump under her arm, which her physician stepfather told her was a lymph node, but Ruth was certain she had breast cancer. She had it biopsied and found, to her chagrin, that it was indeed a lymph node.

Jim said that his wife, Julie, would examine herself until she found a pimple or a blemish to worry about. She would convince herself that it was a malignancy and would run to the doctor for an examination. She remained agitated until the doctor assured her it was not cancer. He said she was always "cranking up" into a major crisis. Jim's attempts at reassuring his wife didn't work, so he decided to take another approach. When Julie would start catastrophizing he would make a cranking motion with his hands, which would cause her to laugh and let go of her fears. Jim suggested that when Julie started to worry, she might ask herself, "How likely is it that I really have this illness? How likely is it that whatever I am afraid of will happen? If it did happen, would it be the end of the world? And, how much benefit is likely to result from me worrying about this?"

PROCRASTINATION MAY CREATE A CRISIS

As a group, adult children tend to procrastinate. They will wait until the last minute to pack for a trip, wait until the guests are about to arrive before starting to prepare the meal, wait to study just before the examination, give themselves barely enough time to make it to the airport, and load their schedules with more projects than it is humanly possible to complete. In many ways, adult children set themselves up to feel pressured and overwhelmed. Unconsciously, they are recreating the crisis-filled environment they were used to as children.

Megan was a substitute teacher and a housewife who grew up in an alcoholic home. She said that whenever she and her husband, Charlie, would go on a trip, he would have his bags packed well in advance, while she would wait until the morning they were to leave to put things in her luggage. She would wait until the last minute to try to pull her wardrobe together and would end up bringing too many outfits because she could not coordinate what she was going to wear. "It always turned out to be a last-minute crisis, and then I would be worn out when we started our vacation." She discussed this pattern with Charlie, who suggested she put her bag out well in advance and daily start putting items she wanted to take in the bag. "It was awkward for me at first." Megan said. "But I found that I did not need as many things, I was able to coordinate my outfits, and I avoided the last-minute panic I'd always experienced." Later, Megan said she made lists on the computer of what she took so she could use them for the next trip to help her organize her packing. "When Charlie and I discussed this pattern, I told him that in my home growing up there was always a crisis. I can see that I was creating a crisis every time we went on a trip." As she thought about this, Megan said she could see how she did the same thing in many situations. She would schedule too many events in a day so that everything would have to go perfectly in order for her to be able to keep all of her appointments. Things rarely did go perfectly, which then produced stress. By loosening up her schedule, Megan was able to avoid the time pressure and risk of crisis she'd experienced in the past. "Another thing I found that I did was to start getting ready for a dinner out at the last minute. It takes me about two hours to take a bath, do my hair, put on my makeup, select my outfit, and to get ready to go out. We would have reservations for seven-thirty for dinner, and I would start getting ready at six-thirty. Charlie would be yelling upstairs asking me if I was ready, I would be tense because I knew we were going to be late, and it would turn into a crisis. All I had to do to correct this was start getting ready earlier."

You can help your companion avoid these situations by encouraging him or her to plan ahead and thus avoid experiencing "time pressure" and these self-made crisis situations. Christie said that Daniel would wait until the morning they were catching their plane to pack, and he would wait to leave until they had barely enough time to get to the airport. Daniel would start studying for an examination the night before the test, and he would schedule clients too tightly, without a margin for interruptions or problems, so every situation was a potential crisis. Christie convinced him to pack in advance, leave earlier for the airport, start studying several weeks in advance, and to thin out his appointment schedule. By relieving the time pressure and leaving some margins for unexpected problems, she was able to help Daniel avoid his self-made crises.

CRANKING UP CRISES

Tony referred to his adult-child wife, Shannon, as a "DQ" (drama queen). He noted that she would take a minor event such as a weather report and blow it up into a potentially major disaster. If she would hear there was a tornado watch, she'd panic. If a blizzard was in the forecast, she would become frightened. Tony's approach was to exaggerate her fears and emotionally flood her with a scenario worse than the one she dreamed up. He named his technique "Exaggeration ad absurdum." If Shannon said there was a thunderstorm warning on the radio, Tony would say, "I guess I had better get out to the shed and start working on an ark." Shannon would protest that she'd heard they might get over an inch of rain, and Tony would answer, "I will build a bigger ark." If Shannon announced a blizzard was coming, Tony would start talking about getting snowshoes and sled dogs. If it was a tornado, he'd talk about stocking the basement with survival supplies. Tony would continue to exaggerate the situation with a smile until Shannon would finally start laughing.

CREATING THE MOST FEARED EVENT

As we have discussed, adult children fear abandonment. In an effort to ward off this feared event, your partner may become demanding and controlling, questioning you about your whereabouts, falsely accusing you of infidelity, misinterpreting your statements and situations in your relationship as evidence of your desire to leave them—all having the effect of pushing you away and potentially leading to a self-fulfilling prophecy in which you decide you might as well leave or be unfaithful if you are going to constantly be accused of it. You can reduce these behaviors by frequently telling your partner that you love him or her as is and that your partner cannot make you love him or her—you just do. Showing your commitment to your companion will dampen concerns over time. At the moment you are being accused, however, it is best to just give your partner a hug, affirming your love and the fact that you are not leaving him or her. Let your adult child know that this is his or her problem and fear. You are not your partner's parent, and you are not one of the people who let your partner down in the past. If your companion raises his or her voice, remind your adult child that "louder does not make it truer."

You Get to Make the "Important Decisions" and Your ACOA Makes the Rest

Sandra was a ACOA who was always on time for her appointments. Her husband, Ken, told us he was allowed to make the major decisions in the family, such as whether or not to "trade with North Korea," while Sandra made the minor ones like which house to buy, which car to buy, and how to raise the children. Sam said he could identify with Ken's statement. As mentioned earlier, Sam's wife, Jill, would ask him a question and nonverbally tell him how to answer by nodding or shaking her head while asking. To help Jill learn to give up control, Sam gave her choices: "Do you want to go to a movie or stay home tonight?" "Do you want me to do the dishes or vacuum the living room?" "Do you want to dine in or eat out tonight?" Jill got to make the decisions, but Sam learned to frame the choices so both had some control over the day-to-day decisions. Sam noted that there was a rigid quality to

Jill's efforts to control. "If we had a nice dinner at Joe's Italian restaurant last week and I ask her where she'd like to go to dinner [this week], she'll say 'Joe's Italian restaurant.' It's as though she wants to latch on to something that worked and avoid the risk of trying a new place."

Even couples with the healthiest relationships occasionally want to control one another. People are like that—everyone wants their own way at times. In healthy relationships the couple respects one another's boundaries and individuality. The partners negotiate and compromise (as opposed to trying to control or manipulate one another) and arrive at agreements and understanding. These are skills your partner needs to acquire. Initially your companion will fear that disagreement is akin to loss of love and the end of the relationship. After your ACOA begins to feel more secure about your love and commitment to the relationship, it will be possible for you to begin to practice the techniques of working through disagreements with him or her.

ADULT CHILDREN CONTROL THEIR FEELINGS, THEIR BEHAVIOR, THEIR THOUGHTS, AND ATTEMPT TO CONTROL THOSE AROUND THEM

Your adult child feels a need to be in control. Growing up, your partner had to at least appear to control her or his emotions, having heard things like, "Stop crying, or I will give you something to cry about." Your ACOA also learned to control her or his thoughts and behavior, and tried unsuccessfully to control her or his chaotic environment. Your partner's parents were either out of control or rigidly in control. As kids, adult children learned to manipulate, and as adults, they are uncomfortable in situations when they don't feel in control, such as flying in an airplane, changing plans, or doing things on the spur of the moment. When your adult child asks you if you want to go out to dinner while nodding the whole time, nonverbally telling you how to respond, you may begin to realize that you are being controlled. In the same way, when your ACOA says, "You are not interested in buying this car, are you?" while shaking her or his head from side to side, you again begin to see that you are not really being asked for your opinion.

Some individuals are good at disguising their control. Nurses, for example, know how to make the doctor think he is making a decision when they are really in control. "Mrs. Jones says she needs something for sleep. She said she used Ambien in the past and it worked." The doctor will then respond, "Give her 10mg of Ambien," and think he made the decision. Had the nurse said, "I think you should give Mrs. Jones some Ambien," there would be no way a doctor would order it because it was not his decision. Some adult children become quite adept at this indirect method of control that isn't immediately detected by the controlee. Some common mechanisms of exercising control are withholding, caregiving, martyrdom, helplessness, lying, and anger. Withholding is not letting someone know what they are thinking or feeling (this may not always be control; adult children may not be aware of their thoughts and feelings). Adult children may control through caregiving by saying, "Look at all I have done for you. You can at least do this small thing for me." Martyrdom is taking on everyone else's problems and then griping about how overwhelmed they feel. Helplessness is denying that they have a choice and getting everyone else to make their decisions for them. Adult children may not say how they truly think and feel, but tell others what they think others want to hear. For example, you ask your adult child how he or she is feeling in the midst of a crisis situation and your partner will say, "Fine."

WHY THE NEED FOR CONTROL?

It isn't difficult to see why adult children feel the need to be in control. As children they had no control over their lives, and now they want a secure, predictable environment. As children they may have prayed that God would help their parent stop drinking, they learned to control their feelings, they were quiet, they tried to be good, they put on a front for the outside world, but they could not control or change the tension and periodic crises that disturbed their homes. The children hoped to avoid parental criticism, having a secret, almost magical, wish that if they pleased their parents, the parent would not need liquor. Some marked the pattern of their parent's drinking on a calendar, at-tempting to predict whether or not major holidays would be disrupted by an alcoholic binge. Their lives remained insecure, unpredictable, disrupted, and chaotic.

Many ACOAs do not like to be passengers. They want to drive and be in control of the car. Similarly, many adult children don't like flying. Jenny was the wife of a busy businessman and the mother of five children who exhausted herself trying to keep her house spotless. Her childless neighbor lady decorated lavishly for the holiday season, and Jenny tried to duplicate the neighbor's decorations in her own home. She decorated three Christmas trees and felt that she was expected to maintain a "Martha Stewart home" during the holidays. Her cleanliness drove her family to distraction. She would jump up to clean out an ashtray if her husband dropped one ash in it. Her children didn't want to invite their friends to their house because she would pick up after them and scold them for messing up the house. Her husband offered to find help with the housekeeping and the children, but Jenny felt that no cleaning woman would be thorough enough to meet her standards and she didn't trust anyone to care for her children.

Jenny realized that her excessive cleanliness was irrational. As a child she was frightened by her abusive alcoholic father and ashamed of their messy house. She did not bring friends home because she did not know if her dad would be intoxicated, and she did not want other kids to see the way their house looked. "I wanted my own home to be a place our children would be proud to show their friends and now, because of me, my kids do not want to bring their friends home." Jenny discussed her childhood experiences with her husband and told him how this related to her compulsive need to clean as an adult. "My home is an extension of me and, in a way, when I clean it, I am trying to keep my feelings under control," she said. She observed that her efforts to control were not limited to her housekeeping. She tried to micromanage her children's and her husband's lives as well. In return, her children were content to let her do their worrying for them. Jenny's insights and her husband's love and support allowed her to let go of her need to be in control. She hired a cleaning lady and also got some help with the children so that she was able to get away from the house and do some fun things for herself. She said she felt so much better once she was able to "recharge her batteries." Her children and husband gave her positive feedback for being more relaxed at home. Her kids began bringing their friends home, and Jenny let them play and did not insist on a perfectly clean house. She was surprised that when she announced that she wasn't going to prepare the elaborate decorations she typically did for the holidays, her whole family applauded. They all agreed that Jenny was improving.

Jeff was a health-insurance salesman and an ACOA. He was married to Gloria, a stay-at-home mom. Jeff wanted his home to be different from his childhood home. He didn't drink. He did, however, attempt to control all aspects of his life. He micromanaged his business affairs and found it difficult to delegate work to his secretaries. He was a compulsive worker and spent long hours at his office and visiting clients. He insisted on a rigid routine at home and told his wife and children how to dress, how to do their hair, and insisted that they keep themselves fit and thin. One morning Jeff got crushing chest pain. His family rushed him to the hospital to learn he had a major heart attack and nearly died. He ended up having bypass surgery. Following his near-death experience, Jeff became recommitted to his faith. His family started attending church weekly, and Jeff joined the men's group and a Bible-study course. His lifestyle changed dramatically. "I learned that God was running the show and that I really did not have control of much in life. I decided to let go and let God. I have had much less stress ever since." Jeff's family supported his changes. They told him they felt closer to him since he changed his lifestyle and became more relaxed. Jeff expressed his letting go of control in this way: "At this instant in time, the world is exactly as it should be; my job is to accept that fact."

HOW YOU CAN HELP YOUR PARTNER

Many adult children feel they have to control the relationship or their partner will abandon them. Since they feel unlovable and unworthy and can't believe that anyone could love them for themselves, adult children strive to make their partners love them. To help your ACOA, affirm that you love your ACOA for the unique person that he or she is, that your love is given unconditionally. Your partner will save a good deal of energy once he or she discovers that your love doesn't have to be earned and that you are committed to him or her for the duration. On a simple level, you can encourage your adult child to try new things and to avoid getting in a rut of sameness. Going to the same restaurant may be safe in terms of it being a known good-quality place, but you miss the opportunity to try new places that may offer something unique and possibly better. You will be helping your companion to see that change can be good and is not something that needs to be avoided or feared.

As adult children look back on their childhood experiences, they can understand that their feelings of being unworthy and unlovable came from the perspective of a child who felt responsible for their parent's shortcomings and inability to quit drinking. As adults they can mourn the loss of unconditional love, attention, and security their parents failed to give because of their alcoholic disease. ACOAs can also come to realize that their loving partners know everything about them and love them as they are—wrinkles and all. Since ACOAs know their partners are good people and know that these good people love them, they come to understand that they must be lovable and worthy as well.

NURTURING YOUR ACOA

One technique we used to use in the hospital in the psychiatric treatment of extremely mistrustful, controlling patients was to sedate patients to the extent that they had to be fed and cared for by the nursing staff. As the sedatives were withdrawn, the patient learned that they could depend on the nurses to look after them. They were then able to let down their guard and be more open and trusting with the staff.

If your companion is ill it will give you an opportunity to look after her or him in order to strengthen your companion's trust in you. As you care for your partner, she or he will learn that to depend on you and that nothing bad will happen when she or he is not in control. So, ignore the objections and baby your adult child when you have the chance.

NURTURING YOUR PARTNER'S INNER CHILD

By now you are well aware that your companion's needs were not met growing up. The unconditional love, predictability, security, validation, attention, and praise that many children receive from their parents was not there because your partner's parents were preoccupied with the addicted parent's disease and had little time or energy to give to the children. As a child, your partner assumed this deprivation was because he or she was not worthy of love or parental attention. Your companion psychologically defended him or herself against this false guilt and ambiguous loss by rationalizing that he or she did not need to be babied, being able to take care of him or herself. And, as you have already observed, your adult child is a survivor.

RESPECT

Your relationship is second only to God in importance in your life. Of course, you will never take your partner for granted. Your partner is humble and self-effacing, though you know she or he is attractive and talented. Why not show your companion the respect that she or he deserves? When someone holds you in high regard, you feel you must behave as though you are worthy of that respect. For example, a second-year psychiatric resident was starting to see patients for psychotherapy. He had little confidence in himself or the importance of this work. The first day he was to see patients, he overheard two maintenance workers talking to his secretary. "Could you tell us when the doctor will be seeing psychotherapy patients?" they asked. "We do not want to be making noise outside of his office that might interfere with his therapy." The resident felt that what he was doing must be pretty important, and he redoubled his efforts to try to do a good job and to live up to the maintenance workers' conception of his work. The same phenomenon occurs in the military. A new lieutenant fresh out of college and reserve officer's training takes command of an infantry company. The master sergeant, who has been in the Army for many years, snaps to attention and salutes. He is respecting the rank, not the person—but it has the effect of making the lieutenant feel he needs to be worthy of the rank and the respect shown to it. By showing your partner respect, you are helping her or him forget the feelings of unworthiness and accept the respect she or he deserves. As you continue to show your adult child respect and she or he accepts it, your companion's identity is being changed in a positive way.

IN SICKNESS AND IN HEALTH

You love your companion and you want to help him or her. You cannot go back and make up for the childhood losses sustained, but you can help your adult child in the present and strengthen your relationship at the same time. As mentioned in the last chapter, whenever the opportunity arises for you to baby your companion and give tender loving care, you should do so, no matter how much he or she protests. Fluff the pillow, make chicken soup, take over chores, and nonverbally show your loved one that he or she can depend on you when the going gets rough. In time your partner will be able to relax and let go of the need to control as he or she depends on you. Being there for your partner when he or she needs support and attention builds trust in your relationship as well.

FEED THE INNER CHILD

Another concrete way to help your partner learn to trust and depend on you is to prepare loving meals for them. People in love demonstrate their love in nearly everything they do. It is the little thoughtful gestures that communicate their affection. Cooking is one way to show your companion how you feel. The little extra things in food preparation and presentation let your partner know how much you care for her or him. This is also a concrete approach to meeting your companion's unfilled dependency needs. Your partner may protest that you did not need to work so hard on the meal or do all those extra things, but she or he loves that you did so. Coming home at the end of the day to the smell of a delicious home-cooked meal and sitting around the table enjoying a meal together are nurturing experiences that help develop an atmosphere of security that was lacking for your partner as a child. In the same way, establishing a menu for each holiday will help your partner overcome apprehension and negative memories of her or his childhood celebrations.

This idea of concretely "feeding" your partner is an approach that is utilized in marital therapy. The high-stress period for most marriages is late afternoon. The husband comes home from work emotionally drained. Psychologically, he wants to be fed and mothered with no further emotional demands. The wife has been home all day with the children (or at work all day and has picked up the children at day care), and she wants to be nurtured and have someone to take over the demands of the children. The children are tired and hungry and want attention from both parents. In essence, all of the family members are feeling drained and want to be emotionally fed. This can, and often does, lead to conflict. If a couple is able to recognize and discuss their emotional needs, they can say, "We are all drained at six o'clock. Let's try fixing the kids a snack and letting them watch something on television while you and I sit down and have a little appetizer ourselves. After we recharge we can help each other prepare dinner and interact with the kids." You are, of course, ahead of most couples in your ability to identify psychological needs, discuss them, and work out a solution to meet those needs.

When you are beginning your relationship together it is helpful to establish predictable routines. Meals can be one of these dependable traditions. Having a certain category of food on a particular day enables everyone in the family to know what to expect for dinner that day. One family followed the following schedule: Monday—Crock Pot or casserole; Tuesday—Asian recipe; Wednesday—soup or fish; Thursday—pasta; Friday—homemade pizza; Saturday—steak; Sunday—either a big brunch or a traditional Sunday dinner with roasted meat, potatoes, gravy, dressing, vegetables, and all the trimmings. As everyone feels comfortable and secure, you can introduce good changes in the schedule. You will find that your spouse and your children resist change once a pattern is established. Everyone likes routine and predictability. Change, even good change, is a little upsetting at first because it is experienced as a loss of the old way of doing things. The new way is the unknown and, therefore, a little frightening.

A SELF-ESTEEM AND SELF-CONFIDENCE CHEERLEADER

The ambiguous losses your partner sustained as a youngster and his or her assumption that the cause of those losses was his or her unworthiness has led to your companion having low self-esteem and low self-confidence. You have recognized the many talents that your partner has kept under a bushel all of his or her life. You can see the great potential your companion has and does not seem to recognize. Your companion is extremely humble, does not think of him or herself as attractive, and does not feel intelligent. Your loved one is hesitant to try to develop or express his or her natural gifts, but you can help.

Over the years there have been some classic experiments in psychology that have shown if people believe they are intelligent, they will do well academically. In one study, teachers were told that a group of students was gifted. The teachers treated the students as though they were gifted, and the students (who were actually average in ability) functioned as though they were "A" students. In another study, a group of male psychology students picked a plain girl on campus whom no one dated and began asking her out. Suddenly her social calendar was filled by a different boy each night. The erstwhile plain Jane began fixing herself up, and when the experiment ended at the end of the semester, she continued to be popular and ended up being elected homecoming queen. Sports psychologists have demonstrated that athletes who use positive imaging perform better than those who do not. Great athletes have already pictured the golf ball in the cup or the ball in the basket before they attempt the stroke or the shot.

Be lavish and specific in your praise of your partner's accomplishments. For example, "Taking that bowl of soup to the neighbor lady shows what a good-hearted, caring person you are." If you praise your partner in front of family and friends, they will chime in and compliment your companion as well. Though your praise and confidence in your partner will help, eventually your companion has to prove to him- or herself that what you are saying is valid. Joyce found this in her work situation when her boss recognized her unrealized potential.

Joyce, the daughter of an alcoholic, was a hardworking, loyal company employee who had worked in a printing company for a number of years. Her boss said that he wanted to promote their business by having a representative go to potential customers and present a program of the services they had to offer. He said, "Joyce, you are the person to do it." "Not me," she answered. "I couldn't do anything like that." "You have been here the longest, you know the business inside and out, you are a people person—you are the one to do it," the boss insisted. Finally, after a great deal of persuasion, Joyce practiced her presentation in front of a mirror at home, taped and retaped her speech, and nervously gave her first talk to one of the company customers. She was surprised at the positive response she received. "I could not believe how well my speech was greeted by the audience. I had more confidence going into the next one, and after a few more consultations, I found that I was starting to enjoy it."

You are in a partnership. We are suggesting that you cheer on your partner to help build her or his confidence and self-esteem, but your companion will cheer you on as well. A relationship should be a fifty-fifty arrangement. Whatever your background, you will need encouragement from time to time as well. A good relationship is better than the sum of its parts. You will both be better people because of your supportive relationship with one another.

IT WON'T BE AS EASY AS IT SOUNDS

You can see that your adult child is intelligent and has many potential skills he or she has not developed or used. You can encourage your loved one to use these talents, but do not be surprised if it is a slow process. David was a young attorney who married a paralegal named Amanda. Amanda was a single parent and an ACOA. David recognized at once that Amanda was very capable in her work. "She could have been an attorney if she wanted to become one," he said. David said he did not push Amanda but wanted to encourage her to use her intelligence and develop her skills in any way that she wished. "My own thinking was that she should go to law school, but I did not mention it. Instead, I asked her what she was interested in doing. She said she always wanted to learn French, and so I got her a computerized French course. She has not opened it to my knowledge. Later, she mentioned she'd like to have a business selling items on eBay, and I bought several books on how to set up this type of business. I do not think she looked at them." David waited a while before he mentioned these situations to Amanda, and then told her that he was confused. "I thought that you were interested in these things," he said. Amanda said that she was, but she had other things on her mind that had been more pressing. "I do not think that's it," David responded. Amanda thought about it and said, "You are right. I think it is part of my crisis orientation. I have never been able to carry through with a lengthy course or project on my own. I have always waited until just before the test and crammed or until a deadline was looming and I had to do it. In these situations there is no real pressure to do it and so I did not—even though I would really like to learn French and how to sell on eBay." David suggested she might want to take both learning tasks and divide them up into short-term units that she could "cram" for and utilize the pattern of study she found to be successful in the past. Amanda said that this sounded like a good idea, but, according to David, she has not started either one at this point.

We give this example because we do not want you to think that changes are going to take place simply or quickly in your relationship. The main point is that you recognize that your partner can benefit from positive feedback regarding his or her abilities and accomplishments. You want your ACOA to know that you support his or her growth, that you respect his or her abilities, and that you are there for your partner when he or she needs you.

YOUR DAILY AFFIRMATIONS OF LOVE

Many adult children read daily affirmations to reprogram the negative mindset they acquired as children. You can do the same thing through your relationship. The small acts of kindness and the little demonstrations of caring are often the most eloquent statements of love.

- Leave a loving card or a poem by your partner's toothbrush or in her or his briefcase.
- Fix your partner's favorite meal.
- Wash your loved one's car.
- Fill your ACOA's car with gas.
- Put a candy on his or her pillow before bedtime.
- Send flowers or balloons.
- Give a small gift.
- Tell your partner how much you love him or her
- Compliment your companion on his or her appearance or on an accomplishment.

These may seem like trite suggestions but they are important. This isn't a one-sided situation; your adult child is very sensitive to your feelings and will no doubt be showing you in many ways how much she or he cares for you. When you think of your relationship, it will be these small, thoughtful things that your partner has done for you that touch your heart.

TOO NICE

Adult children are hard on themselves but bend over backward to be nice to others. This makes them very pleasant people to have around but sets them up to be used by selfish individuals. Adult children's efforts to maintain their façade of always being pleasant and nice keeps others at a distance, because the other people never get to know the adult child's true thoughts and feelings. In fact, ACOAs have a good deal of repressed anger that they are unable to recognize or deal with in a direct manner.

UNCONSCIOUS ANGER

Soon after your relationship began you witnessed some surprising and angry explosions by your ACOA partner. As we discussed, these seemingly furious outbursts were actually expressions of apprehension: fear of abandonment, concern that things were going too well and something bad was going to happen, fear of intimacy, fear of loss of control, and an unconscious wish to reestablish the push-pull type of relationship your partner was used to since childhood. Having witnessed these emotional eruptions, you may be surprised to find that your companion has a great deal of difficulty expressing negative feelings directly.

Brenda was a middle-aged housewife and mother who had sought help for depression. She acknowledged that her father was an alcoholic but denied that his drinking had any significant effect on her childhood, and certainly had nothing to do with her adult problems. She was willing to take antidepressant medication but unwilling to consider counseling or therapy of any sort. When asked about psychological problems, her response was that she was fine. In an effort to convince her that she might benefit from therapy, her doctor read her the results of her Minnesota Multiphasic Personality Inventory. "This patient has a great deal of unconscious hostility." he read. "*What?*" Brenda shouted. "It says that you have a great deal of unconscious hostility," the doctor repeated. "*I am not hostile!*" Brenda screamed. "Okay then, we will just cross that out. We do not want to make you mad." The doctor responded. Brenda started laughing and said maybe she did need to talk to a counselor.

Claudia Black taught us that adult children grow up with the rules "Don't talk, don't feel, and don't think." It is logical to suppose that their angry feelings would be repressed as they tiptoe around their alcoholic parent in an effort to avoid setting him or her off. Much of their childhood experience is frustrating and anger-producing. Since they cannot express their feelings directly, adult children end up with a reservoir of hostility that they can only leak out indirectly through passive means. They avoid confrontation and situations that might lead to a direct expression of their negative feelings. This abscess of anger affects your relationship in several ways and is something you should be aware of so that you can help your partner recognize his or her anger and be able to express it more directly.

WHITE LIES

There is a story about former President Carter's mother being interviewed by reporters. President Carter had given an interview to *Playboy* magazine in which he'd admitted having lustful thoughts, and the reporters were out to get some dirt on him from his mother. They asked her if Jimmy ever lied as a child. She said that, to her knowledge, he never told a lie. The reporters said they doubted this, as everyone told a little lie now and then. Mrs. Carter asked, "Oh you mean like a white lie?" The reporters said yes, that is what they were talking about, and asked Mrs. Carter for her definition of a white lie. "Well," she answered. "It is like when I answered the door and said, 'Come in, I am glad to see you.'"

One trait of adult children of alcoholics is their tendency to shade the truth even when it isn't necessary. In general their deception is not for a selfish purpose but rather to deny problems, deny feelings, avoid confrontation, and to say what they think others want to hear. For example, if you ask an adult child how things are going they will typically answer, "Fine," no matter what traumas they've just endured. As kids they were walking on eggshells, trying not to upset their parents. Ben said that early in his relationship with Julia, he bought her a CD of romantic songs by Placido Domingo. Julia told him how much she enjoyed the music and Ben, being a fan of opera himself, bought her several more CDs of classical opera music. He was surprised to discover several months later that the CDs had never been opened. Julia, at first, said that she just hadn't had a chance to play them but later admitted she did not care for opera music. "Why didn't you tell me?" Ben asked. "Well, I knew that you liked opera and that you were trying to do something nice for me, and I did not want to hurt your feelings." Julia explained. Ben encouraged her to just tell him her true feelings. "I want to know the real you," he said. "I do not expect you to like everything I like—I know we are different people. I love you because you are a unique individual."

MAINTAINING A FAÇADE OF NORMALCY

It is understandable that your partner may have developed some skill in this area as a child. The family denied the parent's addiction, and it was necessary to distort the truth to do so. Feelings were suppressed and family members did not honestly say how they felt. The family tried to maintain a front of normalcy to the outside world, and the information used to support this image was untrue. Your companion was sensitive to the feelings of others because she or he wanted to avoid conflict and learned to say what others wanted to hear rather than the truth. In addition, the family tiptoed around to avoid provoking the alcoholic, and it was sometimes necessary to distort the truth to avoid upsetting the addict. Your partner likely made up stories to cover up for her or his parent's drinking and to explain why schoolmates could not come over to your partner's house to play.

Nicole was an adult child who said that her dad was intoxicated on a daily basis, and her mother was preoccupied with his disease and her own suffering. "They did not pay much attention to us kids. No one knew or seemed to care when we got in at night. They did not care nor did they worry about what we were doing when we were out." Because rules were sometimes nonexistent in many alcoholic homes, the kids made up their own rules based on what they heard their friends say. For example, Nicole told her dates that her parents forbade her using alcohol or being around other people who were imbibing. She later said, "My dad was passed out drunk every night, and my mother was so wrapped up pitying herself that neither one would have known it if I had gone out and gotten blitzed every night. I just wanted to be like the good kids, and so I tried to do what their parents told them to do."

YOUR PARTNER WANTS THE TRUTH BUT DOESN'T ALWAYS TELL IT

You may be surprised to learn that your partner does not always tell you the truth. At the same time your loved one is insistent on hearing the absolute truth and may tell you how angry she or he has been in previous relationships upon discovering she or he had been lied to. Pam was a good example of this contradiction.

Pam was a middle-aged court reporter and mother of three whose father was an alcoholic. She described her first marriage to an alcoholic who embezzled funds from his business, and then left her, the children, and the town where they lived. "My friends told me that he was unfaithful to me and that he was lying to me. I would not believe it, I defended him, and I believed his fantastic explanations. This went on for years until one day I looked into the mirror and I told myself,

'You're a fool.' I suddenly realized that nearly everything he told me was a lie. It was like a door shut in my mind. After that, if he told me that the sun was going to come up tomorrow—I would not believe him. Since being married to that bum, I find that I react strongly if anyone tells me a lie. If I find that someone is lying to me, I drop them like a hot potato." Pam worked and functioned as a single parent for several years. She had a few unhappy relationships until she saw a counselor and began to read the ACOA literature.

It was at this point that she met an airline pilot named Gary who had also been married and divorced. Gary said that Pam told him early in their relationship that she couldn't tolerate falsehoods of any sort. "At the same time, I noticed that Pam would 'fudge' a little herself when relating events to others. It wasn't that she actually lied—she just seemed to put things in a way that would be most acceptable to the other person. For example, I knew she was conservative politically, but if she was around a bunch of liberals she would say things in a way that made them think she thought the way that they did."

FEAR OF CONFRONTATION

People normally disagree in life. Confrontation isn't bad, and it is a common feature in the give-and-take of any relationship. Your partner has a different perception of confrontation based on their childhood experiences in which confronting their parents was out of the question in most cases. Pam said that she and her siblings kept quiet, went to their rooms, went to school, or went to a ball game to avoid the tension and conflict that arose between her parents. "Confrontation to us meant an angry, often out-of-control situation. It was scary. Keeping quiet, not making waves, and getting out of the house worked for me as a kid. As an adult I still get that frightened feeling when disagreements arise. I do not like to be around people who disagree, and I certainly would not want to be in that position with anyone else. When I feel the tension rising, I keep quiet and look for a way to leave."

Adult children avoid confrontation in all areas of their life. They will accept less money rather than ask their boss for a raise. They will tip when they receive poor service. They may be upset if they are kept waiting but won't speak up. At company meetings adult children are reluctant to contradict fellow workers and especially those in authority over them. Pam said, "We'd have meetings at the courthouse with the judge, and he would want to know our opinions about court procedures. If the person next to me voiced a sentiment contrary to mine, I would not oppose it. I usually kept quiet."

Your Companion May Fudge to Avoid Confrontation

Adult children probably don't realize that their efforts to avoid confrontation often involve fudging the truth. For example, if your partner thinks he or she received poor service at a restaurant but still tells the waiter everything was great, your partner has just fudged to avoid confrontation. Kellie noticed this difficulty in her relationship with Eric, who had grown up in an alcoholic family. "We were having dinner, and Eric was griping about the slow service and the poor quality of the food. After dessert, the waiter asked, 'Was everything satisfactory?' To my surprise, Eric smiled and said, 'Yes—it was great' and then gave the waiter a big tip! I said, 'Eric, were you not just complaining about the food and the service?' Eric seemed uncomfortable, but he said he did not want to make a big fuss—the food was not that bad, and the waiter had to make a living like everyone else." Kellie said that this scenario occurred repeatedly in their early relationship. "One time we were waiting for a table and the maître d' asked, 'Do you mind waiting?' Eric, who I know hates to wait, said, 'Oh no, we are in no hurry.' When I first told Eric I thought he had a problem speaking up for himself, he was miffed and defensive. He thought I was accusing him of being 'a wimp.' On another occasion, I jumped in and complained about our service. Eric was obviously uncomfortable and later told me he did not like to make 'a fuss.'"

Assertiveness

You have probably observed that your partner has difficulty speaking up for him or herself, going to great lengths—including saying things that are contrary to his or her beliefs—to avoid confrontation. This is understandable coming from a background where conflict was frightening and something to be avoided. You may have also noticed that your companion becomes uncomfortable when you confront someone and may intervene to try to prevent you from doing so, walk away from the situation, or try to explain your comments to the other person to lessen the intensity of the situation.

Brent said that his ACOA wife, Susie, was very upset with him for sending back his meal at a restaurant. "You are making a scene," she said. "Your steak was okay—why did you do that?" Brent calmly explained that he had ordered his steak medium rare and the steak was overdone. "It was their mistake, and I wanted them to correct it." Susie said that she was embarrassed and shocked at first but, on reflection, observed that Brent wasn't angry with the waiter and the waiter didn't seem upset. "I did not realize that there was something between blowing up and giving in," she said. Susie said that Brent was a good role model for her when it came to assertiveness. "He was always calm and never mean and people did not react to his comments with anger, but he expected good service and would not let people walk over him—the way I always did." Susie said that she attempted to emulate Brent's calm approach and found that it was effective. She was able to get her point across in a nonprovocative way.

This is such a universal problem among adult children (and depressed patients as well) that we established an assertiveness-training course to help patients practice speaking up for themselves in social situations. Adult children tended to perceive even the mildest confrontations as aggression on their part. For example, we encouraged an adult child to tell the nursing staff no if they did not want to do something and to ask for things if they wanted them. The next day we made rounds and found the patient mopping his room. "Did you want to mop your room?" we asked. "No, but I wasn't doing anything, and the nurse asked me to do it," the patient replied. Another adult child who was taking the course said, "I know the night-shift nurses must hate me—I was way out of line last night. I should not have blown up the way I did—I will apologize to them, but I am sure they will never forgive me." We looked at the nurses' notes and could not find a reference to the incident the patient described. When we spoke with the night-shift nurses we were finally able to piece together what had actually happened. The nurse entered the patient's room and shone the flashlight on the patient's face to see if he was sleeping. The patient said, "Would you mind not shining the light on me?" The nurse said, "Sure," and turned off the flashlight. That was the event! The patient saw this as raw aggression on her part. One assertiveness-training alumnus was seen as an outpatient after being discharged from the hospital. She was an adult child who was unable to say no to the demands of others, including her boss. Her employer recognized this flaw, apparently, and told her that he depended on her and needed her to finish a number of projects. The girl had been working long extra hours for no extra pay and her "burnout" was a major factor leading to her hospitalization. The doctor observed that she had a book with her entitled *When I Say No, I Feel Guilty*. "How's the book?" the physician inquired. "I don't know," the patient replied. "I just bought it. I thought it might help me with my assertiveness." When she returned for a follow-up visit, the doctor again asked her how she liked the book. "I don't know," she replied. "My friend asked me if she could borrow it, and when I asked for it back she said no. Isn't that pathetic?" she said. The physician agreed with her that it was pretty pathetic. Another assertiveness graduate made a sweatshirt that had a large "NO" embroidered at the top, then a smaller "no," then a still smaller one, and then "maybe."

Many ACOAs benefit from this formal assertiveness training, but you can help your partner at home by setting up mock situations in which she or he can practice assertiveness.

HOW YOU CAN BE OF HELP

An early discussion of your partner's difficulties with assertiveness may cause her or him to feel that you think she or he is weak and that you intend to reject your partner because of her or his passivity. Therefore, hold off talking about this topic until your partner knows that you really know and love her or him and are committed. Then, as part of your discussion of your partner's childhood experiences, you can explore your ACOA's need to tell people what she or he thinks they want to hear, as well as your ACOA's difficulties with confrontation. Gary and Kellie, as the loving companions, were able to help Pam and Eric, their ACOAs.

Gary explained to Pam why he felt it would be helpful for her to change this pattern. "I told her that I thought it was best to say what you really think and feel. You may lose some friends, but you will end up with people who think the way you do and it is more comfortable." Pam agreed that this would probably be better but said that she did not like to say things that might cause others to think less of her. Gary responded, "When others find out you do not really feel the way you say you do, they will feel deceived. Also, when you say what you think others want to hear, they really do not know you—they only know the image of yourself that you are putting forth." Pam said that she had to think about this and later said she recognized this as a pattern that went back to her early childhood. "Our whole family presented ourselves to the community as something we were not. We tried to be the 'All-American Family' although we knew that our dad was frequently passed out during dinner. Looking back, I do not think we really fooled many people. Most people in town had dad pegged as a drunk." Gary suggested that Pam practice on him. "Anytime you disagree with me, speak up and tell me. Nothing bad is going to happen, I promise. Everyone is entitled to their opinion and I want to know yours."

Kellie said that she and Eric had many discussions about his childhood experiences and his difficulties confronting others. Eric's childhood memories were similar to Pam's. "Children were to be seen and not heard in our family," Eric said. "We kept a low profile and tried to get away when our folks started to get into it." In time Eric was able to admit that he did have difficulty speaking up when he thought the person he was speaking to might not want to hear what he had to say. Kellie said, "My family is Irish, and I told Eric, 'You need to use Irish diplomacy.'" Eric asked what "Irish diplomacy" was. "That's when you tell someone to go to hell, and they end up thanking you for giving them directions." This caused Eric to laugh and say that he didn't know if he could ever achieve that degree of diplomacy. "I told him to practice on me and try to tell me how he really thought and felt rather than what he thought I wanted to hear. He did try to do this and I complimented him when he did," said Kellie. "In time, he got better about telling waiters and service people when he was not happy and, again, I praised him when he did." It takes courage to face your childhood fears and try to change behavioral patterns. Eric said he was improving and that he had been able to request a discount on his motel rates while they were on vacation. Eric related that his newfound ability to bargain was not due to Kellie, but was due to the example set by his friend Sam Goldberg. Eric told the story of how Sam had caused him to change:

> I wanted a radio that I could plug my stereo into, and Sam accompanied me to Goldblatt's Department Store to purchase one. The clerk, who was also Jewish, asked what we wanted and I told him. He showed us a radio for $75.00. Sam told him he'd give him $10.00 for it. The clerk appeared shocked. He said, "See that price tag—it's $75.00. If you want to bargain, go to Maxwell Street." Sam told him he saw the price but he knew what the store paid for it, and they had a huge inventory of radios and if he wanted to unload one he'd give him $10.00. They went back and forth haggling. I was embarrassed and went to the next aisle and pretended to be looking at something else. Finally, the clerk found me, gave me the radio, and said, "There, take it for $50.00." I paid for it and told Sam I had never tried to bargain in a department store in my life and could not believe what he had just done. Sam smiled and said, "That is why God created goys—somebody has to pay retail."

Dennis was a middle-aged businessman who was divorced from his first wife. His children from that marriage were married and out of the home. He married Linda, an ACOA who had been through a series of bad relationships before discovering her problems were internal. Dennis noticed that one unique aspect of their relationship was that they never argued. If they started to disagree on a decision, for example, Linda would acquiesce and agree with him. He would question her if this was how she really felt, and she would say that it was. As time went on and Linda seemed to be more secure in the relationship, Dennis said, "You know that I love you and there is virtually nothing you could say that would cause me to leave you. You told me about your childhood experiences and I understand that you fear disagreement and that you do not want me to be angry with you or reject you, but you are entitled to have your own views on things. When you try to say what you think I want to hear, it keeps us apart, because I never get to know what you really think or feel." Linda agreed it was difficult for her to express her true thoughts and feelings and said that sometimes she really did not know how she felt about things. Dennis said he would try to help her. In their subsequent discussions Dennis would help by clarifying her feelings. "I am sorry I kept you waiting. I did not intend to be delayed but I was. I know that you hate to be kept waiting because it reminds you of the times you were left in the car in front of the tavern by your dad." Dennis also reminded Linda that when she expressed her feelings, she was always correct because only she knew how she felt. Dennis noted that "feelings are not facts. You feel critical of yourself at times and I know that those feelings are not factually correct, but they are your feelings and I would like to know what you are feeling so that I can better understand you and so that we can talk about what is going on between us." Linda said that it was difficult at first to tell Dennis how she felt—especially if she thought he did not agree. But she said, "As time went on I found it easier to express my true feelings because Dennis was so kind and supportive and never got angry with me."

Dennis noted that in the early stages of their relationship he could not get Linda to tell him where she wanted to go to eat or if she wanted to go to a movie. "She would always respond 'Whatever you want to do,'" Dennis said. "It was like pulling teeth to get her to say she wanted to go anywhere. When I finally was able to get her to name a restaurant, she would name one we went to before." Eventually, Linda was able to state her preferences and to initiate plans for their outings. She would say, "Come on Dennis, we're going out for Italian tonight." "I may have created a monster," Dennis said, laughing. "No, I do not mean that—Linda is a wonderful person, and I love it when she tells me what she really wants to do."

In addition to discussing the childhood roots of these patterns and supporting your partner's efforts to change them, you can also be a role model by practicing what you preach. Your partner will observe you saying what you really think and feel and asserting yourself in various situations and will also realize that no one drops dead when you do this; you can still maintain a friendly relationship with the person you are confronting in most instances. In addition, your adult child will see you bringing up your preferences for dinner and entertainment, feeling comfortable doing so.

PASSIVE AGGRESSION

Passive-aggressive is a term that was first used by American military psychiatrists in World War II. It refers to settings, like the military, where a direct expression of negative feelings is not possible and a person can only deal with his or her anger passively and indirectly. The aggression may be expressed in the form of obstructionism, pouting, procrastination, intentional inefficiency, or stubbornness.

Many adult children grew up in an environment where feelings could not be expressed. Sometimes this suppression of feelings was due to fear. Eric, for example, said that his father would scream, "Don't cry," while beating him. Others said that they walked on eggshells at home to avoid upsetting their addicted parent and to avoid conflict in the family. As a result, adult children have great difficulty expressing their negative feelings directly as adults. They fear retaliation, hurting the other person, and being overwhelmed by their rage. The anger is still there, however, and may be expressed passively.

Patricia was a middle-aged housewife who had grown up in an alcoholic home. Her husband, Bob, was a dependable office worker who did little at home outside of mowing the lawn in summer and shoveling the walk in the winter. Patricia was a perfectionist in her housekeeping and was sensitive to criticism—especially from Bob. One morning Bob complained that he had only one shirt that was clean and ironed to wear to work. "What if I did not want to wear this particular shirt?" he complained. The next morning he found that he had no shirts because all of his shirts were in the washing machine. "You were upset by only having one shirt so I thought I better wash them all." Patricia explained. The frustrated Bob looked helplessly at all of his shirts soaking wet, being agitated in the washer.

Donna was a young housewife and part-time librarian who was married to Larry, a construction worker who had grown up in an alcoholic home. Donna said that Larry avoided any confrontation. "He will not argue with me. If he is angry he will deny it. I know he is angry because he stops talking to me. He always agrees to do whatever I ask him to do, but sometimes it takes weeks of constant reminding to finally do it. Other times he does a sloppy job that I end up doing over myself." Donna said she confronted Larry with his passive-aggressive behavior, but he continued to deny any feelings of anger.

RESENTMENTS

Other expressions of unconscious anger are the resentments that your partner allows to fester. Heather was a young ACOA bank teller who was married to Andrew, a young state-employed civil engineer. Heather had been upset when a couple she considered to be good friends of hers suddenly stopped calling and seeing her. She could not figure out why they no longer wanted to be friends, and she could not get a straight answer from them. Heather worried and stewed but, as she discussed the situation with Andrew, was able to conclude that she had done nothing to offend or push them away. Heather was reconciled to the idea that something unrelated to her had changed for her former friends, and she decided to move on with her life and not think about the situation anymore. Then, after several years, her friends contacted her and said how much they missed seeing her and Andrew and how they wanted to get together. Once again Heather was preoccupied with the relationship, but this time she was resentful. Andrew said, "What difference does it make? You liked being friends with them in the past, they want to be friends now, so just be friends and enjoy it." Heather had difficulty letting it go. Andrew said, "Having two friends is much better than losing two."

PARENTING IS SCARY
FOR MOST PEOPLE—
ESPECIALLY YOUR
ADULT CHILD

This chapter focuses on the difficulties adult children have with parenting. When we have referred children to child psychiatrists or psychologists over the years, we have tried to pick consultants who had children—it keeps them humble. We realize that it takes a good deal of chutzpah on our part to be telling people how to raise their kids since we, too, are imperfect parents. We do not expect that you will be flawless either. The purpose of this chapter is to discuss how some of your partner's patterns of behavior can lead to some unique parenting difficulties and how you can be of help. Of course, you will have your own quirks based on your childhood experiences as well. Parenting is scary for most people, especially if they are aware that their own parents were lacking. It is probably one of the most stressful areas of life for adult children.

Here is a good rule of thumb for parenting: do the best you can and do not feel guilty about not teaching your children what you were not taught yourself. In the long run, the only life you really have control over is your own. If you are happy and productive, you will be a good role model for your children. It is also wise to pray to your higher power that your offspring have happy, productive lives. When you make a mistake, laugh and admit it. Talk to your kids about the difficulties you are overcoming as an adult. It is helpful for children to learn that it is okay to make a mistake and that we all have shortcomings that we are trying to overcome in life.

Many adult children feel frightened and guilty about the angry feelings that come up toward their children. This is a normal part of parenting. A few years ago, the news carried stories about children falling or being pushed out of housing-project buildings in Chicago. As a result, the city spent millions of dollars to put screens on the windows of these high-rises. Listeners were calling into the Chicago radio station WLS to express their views about the expenditure of tax dollars for this project. One woman called in and said that she was a nurse who had trained at Cook County Hospital years before. She said, "I can remember, as a student nurse on pediatrics, being horrified to see the injured children who had been thrown from windows by their parents. Now I am older and have children of my own—I understand why they throw them out of windows!"

In the alcoholic home everyone's attention was focused on the addict and both parents were too preoccupied with their own problems to give their kids what they needed. The kids had to take care of themselves and, in many instances, looked after their parents as well. Children in the addicted home lacked mature adult role models with whom they could identify. As a result,, your partner has no frame of reference as to how to behave as a parent and may find books on parenting to be incomprehensible and outside her or his range of experience. Your adult child wants her or his children to have a different experience than her or his own but is not sure what that should be.

Adult children tend to be black and white in their thinking. This causes them to be either too rigid or too soft in their parenting style. They may unconsciously prevent their children from expressing disturbing feelings or thoughts and, in this way, continue the behavioral patterns from their own repressive childhood, or adult children may go the other way, thinking, "My folks were too strict and therefore, I should be lenient." Your ACOA may try to compensate for the rigid structure experienced as a child by being overly permissive with her or his own kids. Your partner may conclude that she or he was deprived, so the right way is to give the kids anything they want. Your companion was not allowed to express feelings, especially negative ones, and may assume that the right way is to let the kids say anything they want. Your adult child may recall that she or he did not have privacy growing up and decide that the children should not be asked anything about their activities.

Your partner's conception of a happy family may have been taken from a family show on television—showing a happy family in which everyone gets along—and may have wanted this. Just as your loved one's idea of a little cottage with a rose-covered picket fence is unrealistic, so are *The Cosby Show*, *Leave It to Beaver*, *The Waltons*, and *Family Ties*. Your adult child may rear a quiet, compliant, respectful, smiling kid who looks good on the outside but who may not have been allowed to express his feelings, thoughts, or to be creative. As one child psychologist remarked, "Parents who want a perfect specimen often end up with a specimen."

TOO SOFT

There is a story about a woman entering a hotel followed by a chauffeur who is carrying a nine-year-old boy on a pillow. "Can't he walk?" asks the hotel clerk. "Yes," answered the mother, "but, God willing, he will never have to." The point is that you can cripple your kids by doing too much for them.

As mentioned above, adult children may strive to give to their children all of the things they missed in childhood and, by doing so, be overindulgent. If they had to cook, clean, babysit, and nurse their parents, they may encourage their children to play all of the time and may make few demands on them. If the adult child was not allowed to express anger, he or she may permit his or her own children to be rude and disrespectful. Adult children tend to be codependent and feel that they have to solve everyone else's problems for them. Alanon has a saying that "the best message carrier in history was Paul Revere. He rode from town to town calling out 'The British are coming, the British are coming' and not once did he get off his horse and help them pack." Adult children do not like confrontation—they are people pleasers. They are self-critical and feel that they never do enough for others. It is difficult for them to say no. They may unconsciously condition their children that the way to get whatever they want from their parents is to keep demanding.

Sharon was an executive secretary who was the daughter of a non-recovering alcoholic. Her first marriage was to Ronald, an abusive alcoholic. When she divorced Ronald she was a single working parent with three children. She then married Dave, a successful real-estate broker who had also been married before. Dave's children from his previous marriage were grown and married, while Sharon's three children were still at home. In her second marriage she was able to give up her secretarial position and remain at home with her children. She told Dave she did not want her family to resemble her childhood experience in any way. Her parents both worked (her father maintained his job despite his drinking), and as a young child, Sharon cleaned the house and cooked the meals for herself and her siblings after school. As a reaction to her childhood, Sharon made sure her children had no assigned chores or duties and were free to play as much as they wished. Without setting consistent limits, Sharon's children, Mike, Ron, and Lisa, did not respect her boundaries. They borrowed her clothing, her car, her makeup, and her CDs and failed to care for or return them. The children took her credit cards without asking and charged things without letting her know. They ran up huge overcharges on their cell phone bills and ignored Sharon's concerns about finances. They intruded on her conversations with other adults. When Sharon and Dave were watching television, the children would pick up the remote and begin flipping through the channels. They were careless with their possessions and when their possessions were damaged, the children would tell Sharon, "My thing broke," which meant, "I need a new thing," "Fix my thing," or "I will take your thing." The children would push Sharon by repeating their demands until she would acquiesce and let them have what they wanted.

Many adult children are overprotective of their children. Dave told how Sharon would chase after their kids in the winter, making sure they had on their gloves, coats, and hats and cautioning them about getting pneumonia. "She was what they call a 'helicopter mother,' hovering over the kids, doing their thinking, and worrying for them. He said he was alone with his son Ron one day when the son walked out without a coat. "You might want to wear a coat; it's pretty cold," Dave told his boy. "Nah," answered Ron. "It ain't that cold out." "Okay," said Dave. "Have a good day at school." That afternoon Ron returned home from school and was shivering and blue. "Jeez, it's cold out there," he said. Dave looked at him and said, "Most guys wear coats on a day like today." Dave said that he never had a problem with Ron leaving home without a coat once Ron realized the consequences for his actions.

Dave and Sharon drove Lisa to college and put her stereo, television, answering machine, phone, refrigerator, and her computer in her dormitory room. They moved her in on a Thursday and classes weren't starting until the following Monday. "What are you going to do between now and Monday?" Sharon asked. "Party," answered Lisa. Sharon's pupils dilated as she imagined the wild college parties her daughter might be attending. "That's fine," said Dave "You just party all you want because we won't be around to watch you. However, you had better make sure that at the end of four years you have a diploma and a way to make a living because they won't let you have your stereo down at the mission." Now it was time for Lisa's eyes to dilate as she was not certain that Dave would prevent her from being homeless.

Sharon was upset that her children seemed to be spoiled and demanding but did not know what to do to help them mature. "I am a terrible mother," was Sharon's response to her children's displeasure or their problems in life. Dave assured her that she was a wonderful mother and had a heart of gold. Her problem was that she was too good. He encouraged her to step back a bit and let the children do their own worrying and assume responsibility for their own behavior.

Sharon noted that the children did not seem to take advantage of her husband and concluded that they were intimidated by his being male and the stepfather. She turned to Dave for advice and support. Sharon and Dave discussed the reasons she had problems holding the line with her children. Sharon remembered being angry as a child because of the deprivation she suffered and the demand that she take on her parent's responsibilities. When her children expressed disappointment or anger toward her, it was awkward for her. She remembered how she felt toward her parents and did not want to be that kind of parent herself, and thus she acceded to the children's demands in an effort to be a "good parent." Dave told her that he was not a parenting expert and that he made mistakes raising his biological children. He said that he was the stepparent with her children and, as such, had to reason with them rather than assuming that they would accept what he said as a parent. Dave and Sharon were able to talk about Sharon's childhood experiences and their influence on her ability to parent. He pointed out that she was bending over backward not to be "the bad parent" and that the children took advantage of this. He suggested that she remain calm when talking with the children and validate their feelings by using "I" statements to describe how their comments and behavior affected her. Dave encouraged Sharon to set limits and establish boundaries and backed her up when she attempted to do so. He reminded her that the golden rule of parenting was "the one with the gold makes the rules." Dave remained present when she calmly told her son Mike that he was grounded until his teacher said he was caught up in his work. "That's not fair," responded Mike. "You don't ground Ron or Lisa when they don't turn in their work." "I understand that you are angry that your activities are being restricted, but it was your responsibility to turn in your homework," Sharon said quietly. "The teacher is a jerk. He doesn't teach us anything; it is a stupid class," said Mike. "He wants you to do well and get the most you can out of the class. Turning in homework on time is important to your success in that class." "I have a date to go to the dance on Friday—what am I supposed to do about that?" argued Mike. Sharon calmly replied, "You will have to tell your date that your mother has grounded you because you didn't turn in your homework." Sharon discovered that it became easier in time to set limits and hold the line on her rules. One technique Sharon found to be helpful and practical was the "broken record" approach in which she calmly repeated her limits to the children. Mike said, "Bob called and asked me to go to the movies with him." Sharon would say, "No, remember I said no movies during the week. Weekdays are for homework." Mike would argue, "Mom, we have been waiting to see this movie. I don't have any homework to do." Sharon would reply, "No, the rule is homework on weekdays. I am sure you have something that needs your attention. Our rule is homework and no movies during the week." "I think it is a dumb rule," Mike shouted as he started to stomp out of the room. "Louder does not make it truer," Sharon remarked calmly. "Most kids think rules are dumb."

As she practiced this technique with her children, Sharon found she was able to establish boundaries for herself with her children and to remain calm while empathizing and even validating their feelings of disappointment and anger. As she held the line, her children stopped pushing her to give in and began to respect her rules.

Sharon developed some innovative techniques of her own. When Lisa asked Sharon for money, Sharon responded, "I am not feeling in the mood to talk about money right now." "Oh, so we have to get you in the right mood to ask for money?" Lisa replied. "Well, when I see that the dishes are not in the dishwasher and your room is a mess, it puts me in a bad mood and I do not feel like doling out money." "If I put the dishes away and clean up my room, will you give me money?" asked Lisa. Sharon smiled and said, "I don't know, but I am sure I would be in a better mood." Dave complimented Sharon on her interaction with the children and supported her efforts to set boundaries and to say no. Sharon made an effort to let Lisa and the boys take responsibility for their behavior. Her ability to say no without feeling guilty improved to the point that she would tell the kids, "What part of 'no' do you not understand?" or "'No' is a complete sentence." Sharon and Dave knew they made many mistakes as parents and weren't always able to be calm and rational in their responses, but their children are now grown and out of the house and appear to be doing well.

TOO HARD

Alicia was a stay-at-home mom who married Boyd, a chemical engineer who grew up in an alcoholic home. Boyd was the oldest child in his family and the family "hero." As a child he frequently had to go to the bars to check on his dad and to bring him home. He looked after his younger siblings after school until his mother got home from work. He cooked, cleaned house, babysat, and was a caregiver to his father while he was still very young. Boyd had a job since he was in eighth grade; bought his own car; paid for his own gas; and put himself through college by working, obtaining scholarships, and receiving student loans. Alicia characterized Boyd as a very loving man but extremely demanding and rigid with the children. He insisted that the children dress the way he wanted, have their hair fixed the way he thought it should be, not be overweight, and get good grades. He assigned chores and berated the kids for being spoiled and babies. He repeatedly told the children how hard he worked as a child.

Alicia told Boyd she knew he did not want his children to experience what he had put up with as a child, but his rules appeared to be for his benefit and not the children's. Boyd felt unworthy and that he never did enough as a child, and his constant criticism was causing his own children to feel the same. Alicia believed home should be a haven for the children, a place to protect them from the disappointments of the world—not a place to dread. Boyd could not wait to leave his parents' home, and his children were starting to feel the same way. Alicia observed that kids from authoritarian homes can't wait to get away and rebel. Boyd agreed that it was difficult for him to compliment his children because he tended to be a perfectionist, and no one complimented him when he was growing up. He also found it very upsetting when his kids disagreed with him or expressed negative feelings. Alicia said, "That is precisely why you are a perfectionist—you need to lighten up on yourself and on your kids." Boyd smiled, "That is why I married you—you help me mellow out." Boyd sat down and explained to his children why he tended to be demanding and critical toward them at times. "You are great kids and I do not want you to feel like I did growing up. I thought if I was perfect maybe my dad would quit drinking and maybe he would tell me he was proud of me. As you know, he is still drinking and I am never going to get his praise, but I am going to make an effort to tell you guys how proud I am of you and how much I love you." Alicia said that Boyd made a concerted effort to loosen up as a parent. "Kids are resilient and when they understood where Boyd was coming from, they realized his heart was in the right place," she said.

CHILDREN GROW UP DESPITE OUR MISTAKES

Alicia pointed out to Boyd that his perfectionism was alienating his children just as he had felt alienated from his own home growing up. She also made an important observation, namely, that children are resilient and can accept the fact that parents make mistakes. Kids *are* resilient and can do well despite our parenting errors. The important points are to focus on the children's primary needs in the family. Give them unconditional love, hug them, tell them you love them, compliment them, and help them develop a healthy self-esteem and plenty of self-confidence. Home should be a refuge from the disappointments of the world. At the same time, however, children need discipline and should respect boundaries. They require responsibilities and to learn to take responsibility for their own behavior. They need to be able to express their thoughts and feelings. As parents, you need not agree with their thoughts or approve of their feelings, but you can validate the latter. This mirroring is extremely important to their later development. ACOAs were not permitted to express their thoughts and feelings growing up and, as a result, have difficulty knowing how they feel or verbalizing their feelings as adults. Reflecting statements such as, "You must be very angry about that," "You seem happy about that," and "No wonder you feel frightened" all help children identify their feelings. You are validating their feelings and letting them know that it is normal to have those feelings.

The teenage years are particularly stressful for parents; they remember their own rebelliousness, and now they find themselves in the role of the mean parent who is restricting their children's opportunity to be independent and have fun in life. Junior high and teenaged kids will often make an outrageous, provocative statement such as, "I don't see anything wrong with smoking dope." Your first impulse is to tell the kid that he's an idiot, but bite your tongue and remember that he is attempting to establish his own identity independent of you. To do so he will make statements 180 degrees from what he knows you think and believe in an effort to be separate from you and to learn from you why you think and feel the way you do. By calmly presenting your case you are helping him learn the reasons for your beliefs. You will be surprised to hear him quoting you to his friends as though these were his thoughts and feelings. Of course, you are going to make mistakes. If you can talk about this with your kids, they will understand that you are not perfect and you don't expect them to be either. Dave told Sharon, "No matter what you do or don't do, there will come a time when the reality of the world will force the child to take responsibility for their own behavior." He then described a situation he had witnessed as a child. "There was a kid in my class in grade school who carved up his desk. The teacher was going to make him stay after school to sand-paper and refinish the desk. The boy's father came to the school and started peeling off fifty-dollar bills while telling the teacher, 'No son of mine is going to refinish desks.' Years later, I read in the paper where the same kid was going to prison for dealing cocaine. He finally reached a stage in life where his dad could no longer bail him out."

It is helpful to have family discussions and invite your children's thoughts and opinions. Alex, a self-employed salesman, and Barb, a stay-at-home mom, decided that a good place to do this was around the dinner table. They developed a ritual that included a regular schedule of menus so that everyone knew what to expect for supper and that dinner would be at the kitchen table at six o'clock every night. The children enjoyed coming into their warm, comfortable house and being greeted by the delicious aroma of a home-cooked supper. The family discussions at dinner were usually focused on the kids and their activities. Barb and Alex felt the nightly ritual helped them all bond as a family and gave the parents an opportunity to praise the children for their accomplishments.

IN THE LONG RUN IT IS UP TO GOD

Raising children is an awesome responsibility, and if you are insecure about yourself to begin with, it can seem overwhelming. Probably the most difficult task for the adult child is permitting the children to express their thoughts and feelings. ACOAs know that they were not allowed to do this themselves, and feelings, especially negative feelings, can be disturbing. Adult children may fear that they will lose control of their own feelings in response or that the negative feelings mean they've failed as a parent. You can help your partner with these difficulties, and, in turn, your partner will help you with your own parenting problems. Through the years of working with hundreds of families, we've seen kids who come from the worst possible homes turn out to be good citizens, and we've seen families where the parents seem to be stable and loving, and the kids get into all sorts of difficulties. The pastor who works with the youth in our church feels that the kids with problems he sees are about equally divided between very poor and very rich homes in town. In both cases, the children are left to their own devices. Affluent children are envied because of their possessions, but their parents are frequently out at cocktail parties in the evening and are preoccupied with their work and social lives.

During the lengthy span of our practice, we have only advised two couples not to have children. One was a schizophrenic man who married a woman he met on a psychiatric unit. The other was a borderline psychotic patient who had been abused as a child and had an uncontrollable temper. Both disregarded our advice and had children. We have continued to follow both families, and the children seem to be healthy and doing well. The conclusion is that although we are proponents of the basics of child rearing, there are many variables involved, and, ultimately, we have to hope for the best and turn it over to God.

ACOAs Frequently Dread Social Occasions

You have been surprised by your partner's emotional explosions when you thought things were going great in your relationship. You have been confused when your partner has become anxious when everything was calm. You may be puzzled as well by your companion's negative, seemingly paradoxical, reactions to what are happy events for most people. In addition, your adult child probably dreads holidays, becoming increasingly anxious as the holiday approaches and impatient for it to be over. You note that birthday parties and other celebrations are met with similar apprehension. Your partner attempts to avoid social events and, when forced to attend, remains on the periphery. Your partner also warns you against having surprise birthday parties or unplanned celebrations for them and is angry if you give him or her a surprise or change plans on the spur of the moment. Your ACOA probably feels apprehensive and self-conscious if games are part of the activities of a social gathering. In order to understand an adult child's discomfort at what most people consider to be happy situations, we need to examine the childhood roots of these adult behaviors.

CHILDHOOD CAUSES OF SOCIAL ANTIPATHY

No one sits down with you as a child and tells you what mothers are like, what fathers are like, how much you can trust others, what you are worth to others, what to expect in social situations, or what to expect on holidays and special occasions. We learn these things through our early relationships. Our memories may not even accurately reflect the reality of our early relationships, but rather how we perceived them through our experiences as children. If you associate crisis situations with holidays as a child, you are not likely to be filled with joyful anticipation of celebrations as an adult.

JOYFUL HOLIDAY CELEBRATIONS

Ask your partner to describe her or his holidays growing up. Chances are your companion will not recall much, and what she or he does remember will be bad. Nancy reported that she thought she figured out the pattern of her dad's drinking when she was a child. "He would drink two days and then stay sober a day. I used to look at the calendar and try to predict whether or not he'd be drunk on Thanksgiving or Christmas." She hoped he would be sober on the holidays but was usually disappointed. Alcoholics Anonymous has a saying: "An alcoholic doesn't have friends; he has hostages." The same is true of his or her family members. They are preoccupied with the alcoholic and his or her illness. Family members hope the addict does not get drunk and spoil the holiday, and they hope he or she does not drink up all of the family's spending money before the celebration. There is constant tension and worry as to whether or not the alcoholic will be drunk and what he or she will do while drinking. Unfortunately, the holidays were often ruined by the tension in the home or a crisis caused by drinking.

BIRTHDAYS, SCHOOL PERFORMANCES, RECITALS, AND ATHLETIC EVENTS

Celebrations, school performances, music recitals, and athletic events are all sources of apprehension for children in alcoholic homes. They wanted their parent to attend just like their friend's parents, but they hoped that parent would be sober and not embarrass the family. Rick said his mother once showed up at a football game with her makeup askew and her blouse unbuttoned, loudly uttering racial slurs, which caused immense embarrassment to him. Rick said he simultaneously experienced relief and disappointment when she failed to attend his games. "I wanted my mom to be there like the other guys' mothers, but I lived in fear that she'd show up drunk," he admitted.

For many ACOAs, birthdays were often overlooked because of alcohol. The father would be intoxicated and the mother preoccupied with his condition or vice versa. Sometimes birthdays were celebrated but spoiled due to adults drinking. Frank recalled that his mother started drinking the morning of his ninth birthday. His father came home from a tavern about supper time and the two intoxicated parents got into a huge argument. His mother threw his birthday cake with the lighted candles at his father. She missed and the cake hit the dining-room wall. "She screamed at me to clean up the mess. That is what I remember from my ninth birthday celebration."

LACK OF SOCIAL SKILLS

Many alcoholic families do not have people over and they do not go out. They do not make small talk. The alcoholic parent may have drinking buddies but "drunk talk" is not a good example of informal social interaction. Children in an alcoholic home do not have social role models. Many watch television hoping to learn these skills from family shows such as the *The Cosby Show*, *Father Knows Best*, or *The Brady Bunch*. Designed for entertainment, these shows do not teach the basic techniques of social interaction; they present an idealized image of family life that is not realistic. Family members in these shows do not have to negotiate with one another or get in power struggles, nor do they repeat their childhood patterns and act irrationally toward one another.

UNPLANNED EVENTS

Life in most homes follows a consistent, predictable pattern. Children know when Dad will be home and when dinner will be on the table.

Surprises and unanticipated celebrations are often exciting and fun, and there is a happy tension and excitement leading up to the holidays. The children listen for the hoofbeats of Santa's reindeer and leave goodies in anticipation of his arrival.

In the alcoholic home, however, there are many unplanned and unscheduled events, but few of them are positive experiences. Some adult children recall trying to protect their mothers from their abusive, intoxicated fathers and being beaten themselves. Jeffery recalled that his alcoholic father had frequently abused his mother.

> She had multiple trips to the emergency room. She had a broken nose, blackened eyes, a cracked rib on one occasion, and multiple bruises and lacerations. The police were frequently called to our house. When Dad started beating us kids, she drew the line and left him. He would continue to call and to stalk her—especially when he had been drinking. One night she called him at two in the morning, when she knew he would be drunk, and told him that he was a fag and could not fight himself out of a wet paper bag. Of course, he went ballistic and came over to our house and kicked in the front door. Mom was sitting in front of the door with a pistol and shot him in the chest as he came through the door. He crawled outside, and she pumped three more bullets in him as he tried to get away. She did not do one day in jail. That is how things were at our house growing up.

ALL WORK AND NO PLAY MAKES JOHNNY A DULL BOY

Many children in alcoholic homes assume adult roles at an early age. It is not unusual to learn that an adult child cooked meals, cleaned, and did laundry at age eight. Older children in the family looked after the younger ones and nursed the drunken parent when she or he needed it. The older siblings might go to the taverns to find and bring home their alcoholic parent. As Barry remarked, "I didn't get to be a kid. After school I had chores at home and, starting in eighth grade, I always had a job. I liked working because it got me out of the house and I got paid. I saw other kids playing games but always thought they were stupid."

Most adult children dread the holidays because they associated them with crisis situations as they were growing up. They lacked adult role models to show them how grown-ups enjoy holidays. In addition, they were probably expected to be little adults and did not learn how to just play and have fun. Because of these factors, it is unlikely that your partner knows how to make holidays fun.

HOW YOU CAN HELP WITH HOLIDAYS

As you listen and empathize with your partner about past holiday experiences, you can validate her or his feelings of apprehension, disappointment, and embarrassment. You can point out that your companion was not to blame for the alcohol-related problems in the home, and you can contrast your ACOA's childhood experience with her or his family life today. While talking about the childhood factors that caused your partner to be apprehensive about the holidays during childhood, you can point out how stable and predictable her or his adult life is presently. Together you can develop your own traditions and rituals for the holidays. Even holiday menus can become part of new family traditions. Help your spouse put a limit to the demands of the holidays so that he or she does not go overboard trying to create a perfect Hallmark Christmas in your home. Remind your spouse that in any family gathering, it is not unusual to have some conflict and some unhappiness; it is not your spouse's job to make everyone happy nor is she or he responsible if someone is not pleased.

Perfectionism is a coping device that is adopted by some children in alcoholic homes. They felt that by being perfect they could ward off criticism and perhaps, magically, parental intoxication. Perfectionism also provides an explanation for some of their adult tension. If the house was in perfect order, if the family would all get along without conflict, if their appearance was perfect—then they would not be nervous. Of course, nothing ever reaches the standard ACOAs set for themselves. As a result, they exhaust themselves striving for perfection and then feel like a failure when it is not achieved. Perfectionism blocks the adult child's ability to develop and express his or her talents. It also gets in the way of the ACOA's interaction with others. The purpose of entertaining is to relate to the guests and have fun with them. Preoccupation with the details detracts from the real purpose of getting together. The story of Mary and Martha in the Bible (Luke 10:38–42) illustrates the importance of relationships over housekeeping details. Martha is upset with her sister Mary, who, instead of helping with the housework and preparation, is seated at the feet of the Lord. Martha says to Jesus, "Lord, don't you care that my sister has left me to do the work by myself? Tell her to help me!" Jesus responds, "Martha, Martha, you are worried and upset about many things, but only one thing is needed. Mary has chosen what is better, and it will not be taken away from her." Because adult children are often anxious in social situations, focusing on the details of cooking, cleaning, and decorating is less stressful than sitting and making small talk with guests. As a result, ACOAs tend to emulate Martha rather than Mary.

ANXIETY, AWKWARDNESS, AND AVOIDANCE OF SOCIAL EVENTS

You realize that your partner lacked exposure to models of social interaction that are a natural part of most children's early experience. You can discuss this with each other and have practice sessions prior to social events in which you help your companion learn the art of making small talk. You can share your experience in social situations. Remind your adult child that most people enjoy talking about themselves. If your partner child asks open-ended questions and listens with interest to the answers, others will regard her or him as an excellent conversationalist. Stay with your partner at the social event to lend support. Afterward, give positive feedback such as "Mrs. White seemed quite taken with you. She said she hoped we could get together again soon." "Everyone said you were lots of fun. I think you were the hit of the party!" Attend more social events as your companion feels more confident. Each occasion will be easier and will help boost your companion's self-confidence.

SURPRISE! UNPLANNED EVENTS CREATE ANXIETY

Alcoholics Anonymous has a saying that needless consistency is the hobgoblin of little minds. It is a reflection of the compulsive personality of the addict. Adult children lacked consistency growing up, and unplanned events were usually bad. As a result most adult children seek consistency and predictability and eschew surprises. If you have a nice dinner at a particular restaurant, it is likely your partner will want to go to the same place the next time you go out. If you cook a meal that is particularly good, your companion will want to repeat the meal. If your ACOA had fun on vacation, she or he will likely want to return to the same spot the next year. Your companion may want to see movies she or he liked again and again. By introducing change, you will initially increase your loved one's anxiety but she or he will be learning that unpredictable events can be fun.

Ed was a middle-aged businessman who married Judy, an aerobics instructor who had grown up in an alcoholic home. Shortly after the marriage Ed decided to throw a surprise birthday party for his new wife. On the pretext of taking her to dinner for her birthday, Ed took her to a local restaurant that was filled with their friends and relatives. Judy was surprised, and so was Ed when Judy told him later that she hated him for setting up this party without her knowledge. She said it was the worst evening of her life, and if he ever pulled a stunt like that again, she was going to leave him.

You can help your ACOA learn that surprises can be pleasant rather than traumatic. Sean knew that his ACOA wife, Tracy, was compulsive about cleaning their home. She did not feel she could leave the house unless it was in perfect order. She was apprehensive about having company because she worried that they might be critical of her housekeeping. Initially, Sean tried to dissuade Tracy from these notions but to no avail. He did some investigating and for Christmas he arranged to have the best housecleaning service in the area come on a weekly basis to clean their home. The woman in charge of the service sat down with Tracy and told her that they wanted her to be happy with their work and asked her to tell them just how she wanted her home cleaned and to give them feedback if their work did not meet Tracy's standards. At first Tracy was a little embarrassed about having a cleaning service and worried that others might think she was putting on airs by having housekeepers. Later, she said this was the nicest present she ever received and she loved coming home to a clean house.

After Tracy and Sean had been married for a few years, Sean arranged a surprise birthday party for her, which she found enjoyable. He subsequently took her on a trip to Florida on a moment's notice. She protested that she did not have time to plan and pack, and Sean told her, "We have a credit card and you like to shop—buy what you forget when we get there." Tracy found that she enjoyed the unplanned vacation. Sean reminded Tracy that we have little control over life's events. He quoted John Lennon, "Life is what happens to you while you are making other plans." It is also important to remember that many of life's unexpected events are good and we do not need to live in dread of what is going to happen next.

LEARNING TO PLAY

Try to interest your partner in taking part in games and sports. Your companion may initially try to be perfect at the game and make work out of the sport. You can show your partner that most games and sports are activities designed to distract us from our day-to-day worries and provide us an opportunity to have fun with other people. Card games and board games can be fun for the whole family or at social events. Glen told Jody, "We tend to be too competitive in the United States. In Australia everyone plays any sport they want and they just try to do their best and enjoy playing, but they do not care who wins. Let's try to be more like the Aussies." Jody was reluctant to take part in a game of charades. "It is silly. I cannot do that in front of people," she protested. Glen encouraged her until she finally tried it. At their next dinner party, they introduced the game to their guests and Jody found herself having fun. "I was actually pretty good at it," she said. "Yes, you were," Glen affirmed. "But there are no winners or losers in charades." Jody laughed and then said with an Australian accent, "I guess you're right; it is just for fun—mate."

IT MAY TAKE TIME FOR YOUR ACOA TO EXPERIENCE FEELINGS IN THE PRESENT

Individuals who experience severe trauma over an extended period of time frequently learn to detach themselves from the experience to protect themselves from pain. This phenomenon is known in psychology as depersonalization. It is as though these individuals are outside of themselves and witnessing (but not feeling) what is happening to them. In time this mechanism becomes automatic. Unfortunately, it is not a selective mechanism and the here-and-now experience of all feelings—not just the painful ones—is lost. Also, the defense continues to operate when it is no longer needed, resulting in the "psychic numbing" that is described in individuals with post-traumatic stress disorder.

Over the years, we have heard thousands of stories of childhood trauma. Kirsten's was among the worst. Among other things, she was an adult child of an abusive alcoholic. When we heard about her childhood we immediately thought of Dave Pelzer's memoir *A Child Called "It."* Kirsten experienced repeated, severe physical, sexual, and psychological trauma. She thought that she must have been adopted because she was singled out from her siblings for mistreatment and because she couldn't imagine parents treating their own children the way she was treated. Later in life she was able to see a number of good therapists and doctors who helped her recover and adjust to adult life. Kirsten married a gentle, kind man who was patient with her and who tried to empathize with her childhood trauma.

One of the last symptoms to be resolved in Kirsten's treatment was her inability to find enjoyment in the present. On vacations she would smile and participate in activities with her family but said that she actually had no feelings of happiness or joy. Later, she could look back on the vacation and talk about how much she had enjoyed it and she said she could anticipate having a good time prior to going as well, but it took many years before Kirsten could actually feel joy in the present. She said that she dreaded psychotherapy sessions because they resulted in her recalling the pain and suffering she had experienced as a child. At the same time, she credited the recollection and reexperiencing of these painful memories as the reason she eventually was able to experience good feelings in the here and now. "It was as though my feelings had been frozen for years," Kirsten explained. "I've finally begun to thaw."

Another patient, Mark, identified with Kirsten's experience. He agreed that therapy might help him reexperience the trauma he was subjected to as a child but said it is too painful for him to contemplate going through it again. Jamie, Mark's wife, said that she plans and selects their vacations because Mark doesn't care where they go or what they do. He is unable to experience pleasure in the present.

Amber related that she was married to Richard for ten years before she was able to experience immediate feelings. She said that earlier she experienced no anxiety when she was in a motorcycle accident or when she watched action movies. Currently, Amber said she is extremely tense when the Chicago Bears are in a close game or when she watches episodes of *24* on television. "A few years ago I would have had no reaction to either," she said.

Understanding this phenomenon is important so that you're aware that it may take years before your partner is able to experience feelings in the here and now. It is only when your loved one has permitted him- or herself to reexperience some of the repressed childhood trauma and, over time, feels safe with you, that your partner will be able to let go of his or her defense of depersonalization and will be able to experience both good and bad feelings in the present.

DANCE AND SING WHENEVER YOU CAN

It is likely that your adult child grew up in a home where the codependent parent worried about what everyone thought. Typically, the family learned to put on a front of normalcy to the outside world and to hide the "secret" of the alcoholic parent. Because of this, some adult children are inhibited about dancing or singing in public, fearing that they "are not good enough" and will be criticized or ridiculed for their lack of ability. Some adult children, however, excel at performing in front of audiences because they are acting a part and do not feel the shame and unworthiness that they feel when they are themselves. For them, acting is a coping device that helps them escape their everyday anxiety and self-consciousness. In any event, it is good for your relationship to dance and to sing with others. As we described in chapter 7, Heather was the daughter of an alcoholic who convinced her husband, Chad, to take dancing lessons. They had fun together, and Chad felt that dancing with Heather produced a tremendous change in him by helping him overcome his inhibitions and loosen up in public. Singing is also fun. Sing in church, at a piano bar, or at a campsite—but sing with others. The difficulty most of us have singing in public may be partly a cultural problem. At the International Tae Kwon Do tournament in Mexico a few years ago, a number of the participants went out for dinner after the day's matches. The participants from other countries sang their favorite songs and invited the others to join in. The Americans had difficulty thinking of songs to sing. They finally ended up with "Home on the Range" and "Row, Row, Row Your Boat." Afterward, the Americans said that they felt uncomfortable because they didn't have songs that they sang regularly. They all agreed they enjoyed singing with the other martial artists.

Once again, your partner may demonstrate paradoxical behavior. Holidays, celebrations, surprises, social events, playing games—all are fun experiences for most people. For adult children, however, they are sources of anxiety. Once you understand the roots of your partner's contradictory reactions, you will be able to help your partner recognize that his or her present life is consistent and predictable. From the security of this current loving and safe family life, your ACOA can learn to play, celebrate, socialize, and enjoy nice surprises.

BIRDS OF A FEATHER

Individuals who associate with one another tend to have similar characteristics. Over the years we have seen that people who become friends on the psychiatric unit or on the chemical-dependency unit generally have the same degree of illness. If one apparently healthy person starts hanging out with someone with serious pathology, we reevaluate the seemingly stable individual.

Likewise, it is important for your partner to realize that his or her problems are not more serious than yours—they are just different. Your companion is not the "sick" one in the relationship while you are the healthy helper. You both have strengths and talents, and you want to help each other make changes in the quirks that get in the way of realizing your full potential as a couple and as individuals in life. Nearly everyone experiences trauma as a child and every person develops defenses that carry into adult behavior patterns. Some of these defensive behavioral patterns produce relationship problems. If you and your companion share your childhood experiences with one another and determine how they influence your actions today, you can sort out the problems that come up between you. Just as you tend to be attracted to others with the same degree of psychopathology, you as a couple will tend to socialize with other couples who share a similar relationship with one another.

FRIENDS ARE GOD'S APOLOGY FOR OUR RELATIVES

We need friends in life. We are attracted to people who share in our growth and lose interest in others who do not. As we learn about our childhood patterns, we find that we do not want to get caught up in our family's unhealthy ways of interacting. It is good to have a loving spouse and good friends with whom we can openly discuss our thoughts and feelings. A joy shared is twice the joy, a pain shared is half the pain. Emerson said that we surround ourselves with the images of ourselves. Just as we pick individuals with the same degree of problems to date and marry, we also end up socializing with people with similar types of behavior. For quick feedback as to the degree of your individual pathology and also the quality of your relationship, look at the people with whom you socialize. If you find that you are running around with a bunch of drunks you better think about your own drinking. If your friends gripe about their marriages and the husbands and wives do not seem to be affectionate or supportive to one another, you may want to review your own relationship. Your friends' behaviors may be a mirror of your own. When you are trying to develop a close, loving relationship, it is helpful to make an effort to socialize with couples who have good, healthy relationships. Observe how they are kind and supportive to one another. Note their gestures of affection. See how much they enjoy one another's company. These are the people you want to imitate and identify with in your own relationship.

Where do you find these people? Your place of worship is a good place to start. People who attend services together typically recognize that they are in need of improvement and are striving to be better individuals. Couples who attend self-help groups are also trying to better themselves. Many couples who work out together in gymnasiums are trying to improve their health and change their lifestyles. Parents who attend PTA meetings and go to their children's activities at school are usually family oriented and trying to be good parents. Couples who take adult education classes together or are involved in a sport together are likely to be compatible and may have the type of relationship you want to have yourselves. Ski clubs, tennis clubs, golf lessons, scuba diving clubs, camping clubs, canoeing clubs, and sailing classes and clubs are all places where couples are trying to develop new skills and have fun together. Many people enjoy camping because they meet other couples who enjoy the outdoors and socializing around a campfire at night. Couples who volunteer for service organizations frequently have healthy relationships themselves and are giving their time and energy to help others.

BE CAREFUL OF YOUR PLAYMATES, PLAYGROUNDS, AND PLAYTHINGS

Randy was a successful professional who was divorced when he met and married Sandy. Sandy was an adult child who had experienced several unhappy relationships and an abusive marriage before her divorce. She was a single parent for several years, and during this period she sought counseling and became acquainted with the ACOA literature. After her marriage to Randy, they attended social functions at his suburban country club. Randy had been a member there for many years and his social life revolved around dinners, cocktail parties, and special events with the membership there. Sandy was the outsider. She described the interaction she observed:

> The men went to one side of the room and the women to the other. The men talked about golf and business. The women talked about where they had traveled or where they were going to travel. They talked about their newest burglar-alarm system, houses in Florida, where they stored their furs, and the recent purchases they had made. They continually told each other how much fun this party was and what a great job the chef did with the appetizers. It was obvious to me that most of the couples did not care for one another and that they were preoccupied with money and possessions. When Randy and I would hold hands or kiss one another, it made them uncomfortable.

Randy said he had known these people for many years and thought they were good people, but he agreed with Sandy's assessment. There seemed to be a superficial preoccupation with the material values of the world and not-so-subtle scorekeeping.

Randy said, "I realized what Sandy was saying about these people. We did not fit with them at this stage in our lives." Sandy did not enjoy going to events there, the children were not using the club, and he decided that he had changed and now felt out of place with his former social group. "They are the same good people, it is just that my relationship with Sandy and the kids is of utmost importance to me at this time in my life. I think my old buddies played golf all of the time to stay away from home, and I did as well. Now I had rather be home than on the golf course," Randy said. He withdrew from the club a few months later.

During their discussion of the country-club marriages, Randy said that it seemed to him that a good many of the couples were staying together for financial reasons. Randy told Sandy the story of the couple who were having dinner at the club when a beautiful young woman walked up to their table and gave the man a warm embrace and a kiss on the cheek. When she left, the wife asked, "Who was that?" "Oh, that was my mistress," the husband replied. "Your mistress!" the wife exclaimed. "I'm calling a lawyer Monday and we're getting a divorce." "Well," answered the husband, "you could do that, but we'd have to move out of our house by the club, you wouldn't be able to have a cleaning woman or a maid, and you would probably have to get a job." Just then, an older gentleman with a young, beautiful girl walked by their table. "That's not his wife," the woman exclaimed. "No, that's his mistress," the husband explained. The wife smiled with self-satisfaction. "Our mistress is better looking than theirs."

STICK WITH THE WINNERS

You have a head start on many couples because of the way your relationship began. Your adult child made a conscious effort to find a dependable person like you who is capable of having a close, lasting relationship. You began to understand their childhood experiences and how they resulted in the sometimes confusing and paradoxical adult behaviors that you were beginning to experience first hand in your relationship. You, in turn, began to share your own childhood experiences with your partner, who helped you understand your own set of adult behavioral quirks. When problems arose between you, you were able to sit down and discuss what had happened and determine the underlying emotional roots of the conflict. This process that you have gone through together has resulted in your having a much closer and deeper relationship than most couples experience.

You may be fortunate enough to find other couples who share this deep awareness and who are capable of discussing the childhood roots of their behaviors. Not that you would want to sit around and discuss these things socially, but it will be comfortable for you to be around friends who have a deep understanding and love for one another. It is easy to tell if a couple has a good relationship. Just ask them, "How is your relationship?" Those who have good ones will answer immediately and say something like, "Great," "It could not be better," "She or he is the love of my life." Those with shaky relationships will start tap dancing, "Well, we have our ups and downs like every relationship," "We have been together a long time," or "Pretty good." You can spot a couple in love by the way they interact with one another. They stay close to one another, look into each other's eyes, and touch each other. It is obvious they enjoy talking to each other, and they appear to be best friends. The next time you are in a restaurant, look around at the couples dining there. See how many good relationships you can spot. We have done this over the years and have been surprised at how many couples go out to eat and do not speak to or look at one another throughout the meal.

The point is you want to be in the company of couples who are in love with each other and who enjoy their association. These are men and women who are best friends. They like to be around one another and they enjoy talking with one another whether they are at home or out at a restaurant. You will feel comfortable around this type of couple because you love and enjoy being with your spouse as well. Neither you nor they will become upset by showing affection for one another. Their demonstrations of affection will inspire you to be loving and respectful to your partner.

SOME COUPLES ARE UNABLE TO INTROSPECT YET STILL DO OKAY

We have emphasized introspection and analysis of each other's behavior. We feel this process results in a deeper and more interesting relationship, but this is not always true for everyone. Some people find it too difficult to rehash the trauma of their childhood experiences. A Delta Force officer who had extensive combat experience in Vietnam told us that he gave his officers the following advice regarding introspection: "Everyone carries a sack of manure [he used a more explicit term] on their shoulders—your quality of life depends on how often you stick your head in that sack." Some people are not capable or willing to explore themselves. Despite this, many of these individuals can have good relationships.

James was a farmer who grew up in an abusive alcoholic home. He left home when he was twenty to move in with Liz, a twenty-two-year-old schoolteacher, who was also from an abusive alcoholic home. He said that both of them found it upsetting to talk about their childhood experiences. They both wanted to forget the past and to have a nice, loving family that was safe and secure. James said, "We comforted each other, never raised our voices, shared a common faith, and always have had a good marriage." Liz said they were proud of their children, who all seem to be happy and doing well in their adult lives. Neither Liz nor James could tolerate much anger or confrontation because of their abusive childhood experiences, and they became anxious if they felt anger themselves. No doubt these feelings were suppressed in their own family. Nonetheless, they said they were happy and they appeared to be happily married. They said their children were happy and doing well, and this also appeared to be true.

As James and Liz demonstrate, there are individuals from dysfunctional backgrounds who are not psychologically minded and who do not introspect. Despite these shortcomings, they are apparently able to have good relationships and happy lives. In the case above, the couple just consciously made up their minds that they were not going to be like their abusive parents and were going to respect one another. We mention this because we want to acknowledge that following our recommendations is not an absolute condition of marital happiness. Some people take another route and still end up being happy with one another and their relationship. We are not recommending this approach, but we have to acknowledge that some people who fail to introspect have been able to work out happy relationships for themselves and appear to be content with themselves and with their families.

TENDING TO YOUR RELATIONSHIP

Your relationship is one of your top priorities; it is basic to your happiness in life. Therefore, you want to make sure that you nurture it daily and help it continue to strengthen and grow over time. Be certain that you allot time for your relationship each day. Recognize its importance and do not neglect it because of life's other demands. Drop other commitments if your relationship needs attention.

Let us review your relationship as it stands. You are both aware that you cannot change your partner, but, with effort, you can change yourselves. You have learned to talk about yourselves and to express your feelings to one another. You listen to each other nonjudgmentally and empathize with each other's childhood experiences and feelings about those events. You have acquired the ability to analyze each other's adult behavior patterns. Through your partnership, you have been able to resolve conflicts, establish boundaries, and negotiate compromises.

Your goal is slow and steady growth. As they say in Alcoholics Anonymous, "Inch by inch it's a cinch; yard by yard, it's hard." A relatively small amount of money invested on a regular basis will grow into a fortune in time, and small daily investments in your relationship will do the same. Change and growth occurs as the result of daily practice. If you do anything for one hour each day you will become good at it. If you exercise each day, eventually it will pay off, and if you lose a few ounces of weight each day, your weight loss will be significant in a year. Likewise, your relationship will improve on a daily basis as you handle problems together, share with one another, support each other, and show your love through small kindnesses and intimacies each day.

GENERAL PRINCIPLES

You cannot make anyone love you—love is a gift that must be given freely. You would never knowingly do or say anything that would hurt your partner. However, it is almost impossible to avoid inadvertently hurting him or her on occasion. Should you talk or act in a way that upsets your companion, you should be quick to apologize for your mistake. Do not make excuses or try to shift responsibility. Instead, let your loved one know you will try to do better. For example, "I know that it bothered you last night when George helped his wife with her chair at the table, and I just sat down. I knew that I erred the minute I did it. I hope that you will accept my apology. I promise to be more courteous the next time we go out—in fact, I am going to start practicing at home."

Never take your partner for granted. Do not forget to compliment them; everyone likes flattery. Your adult child probably did not get much positive feedback during her or his formative years, and compliments are especially welcome coming from her or his favorite person in life. Be specific with your praise by pointing out the particular attribute or behavior you admire. For example, "Your centerpiece is beautiful; you have a real talent for flower arrangements." "You look sharp. I like the way your blue suit brings out the blue of your eyes." "Taking that bowl of soup to Mrs. Jones was very thoughtful; you have a kind heart."

One-upsmanship and competition have no place in a good relationship. Keeping score in terms of who did the most or who made the most mistakes is also verboten in a healthy union; these practices are absolutely wrong in a relationship with an adult child. Your adult child probably already has low self-esteem and tends to feel that he or she comes up short in any comparison. Your partner will likely agree that he or she is inferior to you and will expect you to be disappointed in him or her. Your role is to not let your adult child put him or herself in a one-down position in the relationship. You want to look for opportunities to compliment your companion and help increase his or her self-confidence.

Reggie grew up in an academic family. He married Valerie, who was an unassuming and modest adult child. Reggie said that his family of origin would sit around the dinner table and try to "one-up" each other by quoting articles, using foreign phrases, and stating trivial facts to demonstrate their superior intelligence and knowledge. At first he found himself doing the same thing with Valerie, who was deferential and complimentary about his fund of information. "Then it dawned on me—this was my problem and a carryover from my childhood. It was stupid to try to impress someone you know loves you for yourself. I apologized and told Valerie to call me on it when she saw me getting into the Stephen Potter thing." George and Martha in *Whose Afraid of Virginia Woolf?* carried one-upsmanship, keeping score, and belittling one's partner to the ultimate limit.

The same problem can carry over into family games. The object of a family game is to have fun together—not to win. Edward was an adult child who did not have an opportunity to play growing up. He was his family's hero who became a workaholic as an adult. When he took up a sport he first read about it, then he took lessons, and then he drilled until he reached what he felt was an acceptable level of competence in the sport. His spouse, Cynthia, pointed out to him that he converted a recreational sport into a job by the time he was finished with it. She encouraged him to take up noncompetitive activities such as yoga and fishing with a cane pole, bobber, and worm.

Focus on the positive aspects of your partner and your relationship, and minimize the negative. Any two people who live together for a period of time will begin to experience irritation with some of the habits of their partner. They will be able to predict their mate's behavior, know that they are going to repeat some annoying phrase or action, and then resent it when they do. These are things that can be discussed when you are both feeling good about yourselves and each other. For example, Matt told his partner, Rebecca, that she always left the vent running in the bathroom and he found this annoying. "I know it is a little thing, but I am continually turning it off and I worry that it will burn out the fan motor." Rebecca thanked him for pointing this out and said, "I did not know that I was leaving it on, nor that it bothered you, but I will make a conscious effort to turn off the vent." Rebecca did her best to turn off the vent, and Matt appreciated her effort in this regard. She later told him that he continually used the phrase "Git-R-Done," which she found tiresome. "It was funny at first, but now it is boring. I wish you would think up something new to say," she said. Matt said that he did not realize he had been overusing the phrase or that it bothered Rebecca but promised to try to find another phrase. "I used to say 'Yada, yada, yada,' and I guess when I dropped that one I started using 'Git-R-Done,'" he said.

These are small irritations, but if left to fester, they can grow into major annoyances in the relationship. In a good relationship, such as Matt and Rebecca's, the partners are each able to listen to the other without becoming defensive and are willing to make changes in their own habits at their partner's request. They do this because they respect their companion's wishes and do not want to cause any negative feelings if they can help it.

HELP EACH OTHER GROW AS INDIVIDUALS

You will naturally want to spend time together and be with one another, but you will also want to encourage your partner to recognize and develop her or his own interests and talents independent of yours. Involvement in independent pursuits does not mean a distancing of your relationship nor does it imply less intimacy between you.

Your companion may underestimate his or her abilities. This kind of perfectionism may block the expression of your partner's talents. Encourage your companion to try new things and to learn new skills without attempting to grade his or her efforts. Jonathan, a martial artist, was married to Mindy, who was an adult child. He explained the initial learning process that everyone goes through when taking up a new interest: "Everyone starts out as a white belt in a new activity. That is part of the fun of learning something new. First you are awkward and feel inadequate, and then you develop a false sense of competency."

Your adult child may neglect her or his own health while trying to take care of everyone else. Try to help your partner take care of her or himself as well. You might want to remind your loved one that people are like batteries: if everything is going out and nothing is coming in, a person will soon be drained. If your companion is burned out, she or he will not be of much help to anyone else. Therefore it is not selfish for your partner to include gratifying activities that improve her or his own health and restore spent energy.

Your happiness, or unhappiness, does not depend upon your companion's and vice versa. Independent interests and activities do not take away from the closeness of your relationship. As you grow as individuals your relationship will change, so reassure your partner that change does not mean loss or even a distancing of the relationship. Change is not a bad thing; it is part of life and it is what you want to happen in your relationship. In a healthy relationship both individuals have room to develop and reach their full potential in life. This can be threatening to the non-ACOA if he or she is codependent.

An example of how an ACOA's growth and development ended her friendship with two codependent friends was illustrated by Lauren's relationship with an older couple, Jane and Phil. Lauren was an ACOA and a single parent who was married to an abusive alcoholic. She later determined that she had picked him because of an unconscious attraction to someone who reminded her of her father. An older couple, Jane and Phil, helped Lauren through the stress of her divorce. They supported her emotionally, and their home became a nurturing oasis for Lauren and her kids. The older couple looked forward to their visits and became surrogate parents for Lauren, who looked up to them and asked their advice on many day-to-day problems. Lauren would call Jane at least once a week to share the week's events and to listen to her suggestions about day-to-day problems.

Meanwhile, without Jane's help, Lauren read ACOA literature and got into counseling. She met Rod, a nice, stable professional, and shared her childhood experiences and the influence they had on her adult behaviors. Rod listened, empathized, and shared his own experiences with her. Their relationship blossomed and they married. With their combined income and Lauren's advancement in her own career, Lauren's financial situation improved significantly. Lauren noted that Jane and Phil seemed to distance themselves. They stopped calling and visiting, and they no longer offered invitations to Lauren and her family. Lauren later learned that they had "adopted" a young single parent who was having financial difficulties. Jane was baking for the family, having them over for meals, and advising the young woman on her everyday problems. At first Lauren was hurt that her surrogate parents abandoned her. She discussed this change with Rod and concluded that, in a way, this was the result of Lauren's making positive changes in her life and her growth in independence and confidence. Jane and Phil had a need for a certain type of relationship and when Lauren became more independent, she no longer met their caregiving desires and they moved on to help a person who was in greater need of their nurturance.

The same type of problem can arise in a marriage if the spouse of the ACOA is codependent and has a need to take care of his or her partner. The partner may thwart the adult child's growth or, at least, not encourage it. The partner may also feel that the adult child's independence means that he or she no longer needs or loves the spouse as a partner. This is why we encourage you to support and encourage your adult child to grow and develop as an individual. It is good to introspect and try to improve your own shortcomings, but try to abstain from attempting to "fix" your adult child's problems for him or her.

A GOOD RELATIONSHIP IS STRONGER THAN THE SUM OF ITS PARTS

A corollary to encouraging one another's independent development is to defer to your partner's superior talents and learn from her or him. If your companion knows more about decorating or gardening, for example, give her or him the lead in those areas and learn from your partner. By sharing your unique abilities with one another, you will both grow and become better people. As a general rule, women are better at expressing their feelings. If this is the case in your relationship, let your wife help you identify and express yours.

Talents are not always gender specific. Helen was an adult child of an alcoholic who married Fred late in life. Helen liked to garden and do yard work. She had raised her children as a single parent and said that she was tired of cooking. Fred had medical problems that precluded strenuous activity. He developed an interest in cooking and had become a gourmet chef. Fred said, "I guess there is a little role reversal going on at our house. I am in the kitchen working on dinner while Helen is outside mowing the lawn. It works for us. We are both happy doing what we are doing."

Because you are secure in your partner's love, you are able to listen to suggestions and criticisms from him or her without becoming defensive. This enables you both to learn from your mistakes and weaknesses and grow as individuals. Allison was an adult-child homemaker who was married to a businessman named Troy. Allison insisted that Troy follow a diet and begin an exercise program. "I am too fat," Troy acknowledged. "If anyone else told me I needed to lose weight and to get in shape, I would probably become defensive and point out something they needed to improve as well, but I know that Allison loves me and has my best interests at heart. I realize that she is concerned that I will develop health problems and she wants me to live as long as possible—and I want to be with her as long as possible, too—so I listen and try to do what she says."

KEEPING THE RELATIONSHIP INTERESTING

In the past, your adult child sought the exciting roller-coaster eros brand of love, finding reliable, steady individuals to be boring. Your loved one may have experienced a few bad relationships before coming to the realization that she or he was recreating a childhood pattern and made a conscious effort to establish a relationship with a reliable person like you. The relationship need not be boring, even though you are not creating periodic crises in their lives.

Humor is a way of introducing a positive unpredictability into the relationship. Surprise is the essence of any joke. For example: Two women were traveling through the South. They saw a sign outside of a town that said "Bon Temps." They thought this was an unusual name and were not sure how to pronounce the name of the town. They went into a local restaurant and said to the waitress, "We would like to know the name of this place, but please pronounce it clearly and carefully so that we can understand." The waitress said slowly, "Bur-ger King." The surprise of the waitress clearly pronouncing the name of a well-known chain restaurant instead of the exotic name of the town produced the humor. This is a type of surprise that is funny and pleasant rather than the traumatic surprises that most adult children experienced in their early years.

Comedy is a means to enliven and lighten your relationship. As you grow to know one another better, you will become aware of the origins of each other's adult patterns of behavior. Each of you will no doubt want to modify some of these carryovers from childhood, and it is so much easier if you can kid one other about them and laugh at yourselves when you make mistakes. Jason, an adult child, woke up worrying about whether to get a sedan or an SUV for his next automobile purchase. He continued to bring up the topic and to list the pros and cons over and over. His wife, Gladys (who he referred to as "happy bottom"), pointed out that things had been going very well in their lives, and it seemed to her that he was trying to crank up a crisis by worrying about something that did not really make a great deal of difference. Jason laughed and said she was probably right. He agreed he should count his blessings and stop obsessing about automobiles.

DEALING WITH
ADDICTION PROBLEMS

Your partner is at risk for the disease of alcoholism and chemical dependency. Should your loved one show signs of addiction, you do not want to baby or enable her or him, but people often need love the most when they are the least lovable. As we will discuss, you want to affirm your love for your partner but also communicate that the addiction is his or her problem. You also want to determine what your own limits are in this regard. Will you stay with an ill person who refuses to acknowledge his or her illness or seek help? Will you tolerate the virulent damage that addiction will surely do to your relationship?

After growing up in the traumatic atmosphere of an alcoholic home, you would expect that an adult child of an alcoholic would abstain from alcohol and be against anyone drinking in the home. Some adult children do just that. As we have seen, however, others are attracted to alcoholics and repeat the roller-coaster relationships they knew as children. Many, surprisingly, become "bibacious" themselves.

Sixty percent of all alcoholics had an alcoholic parent and are also adult children of alcoholics.

YOUR PARTNER IS AT RISK FOR ADDICTION

Adult children of alcoholics are predisposed to substance (ingested) addictions such as alcohol, drugs, and food. They are also prone to process (activity) addictions such as gambling, work, shopping, sex, religion, or addictive relationships. A number of environmental and social factors may help predispose them to these problems. Will reported that his abusive alcoholic father had been a distributor of dairy products when he was growing up. "He would come home drunk and beat up mom. My little sister and I would hide in the field until he passed out and then go in and try to take care of our mother. The next day he would bring home ice cream for all of us kids." Will said that one way he coped with stress in his adult life was by compulsively eating ice cream. "I always keep some in the freezer and whenever I feel stressed I pig out. Whatever happens in life I feel I can make it as long as I have a supply of ice cream."

Adult children suffer from early ambiguous losses and from "frozen grief." They are poisoned with toxic shame. They have trouble asking for help from others; tend to keep their problems to themselves; experience high levels of chronic tension; are uncomfortable in social situations; are critical of themselves; and may self-medicate with alcohol, drugs, or food for a temporary solution for these problems. Adult children may identify with their addicted parent and see alcohol as a way to cope with life. In addition, there are genetic factors to be considered. Because a person has a genetic predisposition for alcoholism doesn't mean that she or he has to become an alcoholic; it means that individual has to be more guarded than someone who isn't so predisposed. The Irish, Native Americans, and Aborigines are known to be more prone to alcoholism and, as a result, should be more cautious about drinking. Some Asian races cannot tolerate alcohol well and experience an uncomfortable flushing after ingesting a small amount. Research shows that Asians are able to overcome this reaction and become addicted as well.

Alcoholics Anonymous says that being restless, irritable, and discontented leads to drinking in an effort to self-medicate these symptoms. Dr. Abraham Twerski, who is a psychiatrist and a rabbi, feels that a failure to meet the spiritual needs that every human has leads to a vague unrest that the individual may try to quiet chemically. Some people become addicted because of their efforts to self-medicate and cope with stress.

Tim was an advertising executive who had grown up in an alcoholic home. He was happily married to Janette, a bookkeeper who liked orderliness and predictability in her life. Tim had visited his college roommate's home during their school years and had noted that they seemed to be a happy, loving family. His roommate's father cooked out on the grill, and both he and the mother had a couple of cocktails before dinner. Tim said that this scene of a happy family cooking out and enjoying cocktails together stuck in his mind as to how he wanted his future family to be. Tim and Janette followed this formula after their marriage, and it became a ritual for them to enjoy two cocktails together each evening. Over time, Tim's consumption increased from two to several drinks each evening while Janette's remained the same. When they went out to dinner, Tim would have several strong drinks at home before leaving for the restaurant. In the establishment dining room, he would tell the waiter he wanted to relax before ordering dinner and would drink several more cocktails before placing his order. During dinner he would have one or two bottles of wine and then have several after-dinner drinks. When Janette asked about going home, Tim would become irritated and refuse. "I am enjoying myself and I have not finished my drink. You can go if you want—I will take a cab," he would reply.

When Janette mentioned the increase in Tim's consumption, he pointed out that she had put on some weight and he had refrained from commenting on this. Tim's drinking continued. He passed out at two family cookouts, wrecked Janette's car, and fell through the shower stall in the bathroom, where Jeanette found him in a pool of blood and glass. Tim was picked up for drinking while driving and refused to be tested. Tim stayed up all night drinking and was unable to get up to go to work several Mondays in a row. Tim and Janette's children were grown and out of the house, but they noticed and commented on Tim's drinking. He responded with irritation. Although Janette did not lie or cover up for Tim, she did not take any action because in the past when she had confronted him he blew up and threatened to leave. Janette sought help for herself and read some of the literature on alcoholism. She learned that she could not control Tim's drinking nor could she make him change his behavior. She learned to take care of herself and emotionally detach herself from Tim's addiction.

Tim's drinking continued to increase. He was careless about his appearance, his occupation, and his chores at home. One night he urinated in the closet and then denied doing it the next day. Janette realized that he had experienced a blackout. She consulted with a chemical-dependency unit counselor, who suggested an intervention. The counselor explained that confrontation by the family and his employer might enable Tim to get help before he lost everything and hit bottom. The term the counselor used for this was *high bottom*. Janette contacted the children, Tim's mother, and a representative from the company where he worked, and they scheduled a meeting with the chemical-dependency counselor on the rehabilitation unit of the local hospital. They told Tim they were meeting to discuss his drinking. Out of curiosity, Tim came to the meeting. The family members told him that they loved him and then confronted him with their observations. His company representative presented his observations of Tim's increasingly frequent absences from work, as well as his personal observations of Tim's behavior at company social events.

At first Tim was angry and defensive, and he pointed out each of the family members' problems. They say in Alcoholics Anonymous, "We have a disease that tells us we don't have a disease." Tim then said he would abstain from alcohol on his own and that there was no way he could go into a rehabilitation unit at this particular time. The family responded that they had already made arrangements with his business and with the hospital, and they were going to accompany him to the unit that day. The company representative said that rehabilitation was a condition to the company's permitting Tim to return to work. Tim reluctantly accepted the decision. He completed the required inpatient stay and has continued to attend Alcoholics Anonymous on a daily basis, see his counselor, and talk with his sponsor. He has remained sober. Janette attended family meetings and, although she knew this was not a requirement, decided that she would also abstain from using alcohol. She and the kids cleared the house of alcohol while Tim was on the inpatient unit.

Tim and Janette agree that things have been much better since the intervention, but they have had to find new friends who are not drinkers. They have become more involved with their church. They both know that Tim is still an alcoholic who is only one drink away from a relapse and that they must continue to be vigilant and to work the Alcoholics Anonymous twelve-step program. From their involvement in Alcoholics Anonymous they learned that certain times and situations can precipitate drinking, drug use, smoking, eating, or other compulsive behaviors by adult children of alcoholics. Identifying these "triggers" can help an alcoholic control his or her urge to indulge. The acronym HALT stands for hunger, anger, loneliness, and tiredness; these are the states that may weaken an individual's resolve and make one more vulnerable to addictive behavior. Often, there is cross-addiction and some individuals will stop drinking only to get into trouble with compulsive gambling, sexual behavior, drug use, smoking, shopping, eating, or working.

The example above of pressuring the unwilling alcoholic to seek treatment before she or he hits absolute bottom may seem unduly coercive to readers unfamiliar with addiction. You are correct—it *is* coercive, but it is also necessary and it works in many instances. Dr. Bey initiated an alcohol treatment program at Fort Knox during his Army service in which soldiers were referred by their commanding officers, the military police, or emergency-room doctors who recognized that these individuals were addicted to alcohol. This so-called voluntary treatment program consisted of the soldiers taking Antabuse daily for six months, attending an Alcoholics Anonymous group daily, and having group therapy three days a week for six months. Failure to comply with any of these requirements resulted in reprimands for the first two offenses and expulsion from the military without benefits the third time a soldier failed to comply. The soldiers in this program complained initially. "You call this a voluntary program?" they would say. Dr. Bey would smile and respond, "Well, it is *sort* of voluntary." However, it was gratifying to see later that nearly all of the participants did complete the program, remain sober, and continue to attend Alcoholics Anonymous. Many of these men, and their families, thanked the staff for forcing them to get help.

THE ROLE OF MEDICATION IN THE TREATMENT OF ADDICTION

Of course, not all alcoholics go into rehabilitation or Alcoholics Anonymous. Some quit drinking on their own. Some enlist the help of medicines that are available to reduce craving (ReVia), prevent the use of alcohol (Antabuse), or restore the balance of neurotransmitters in the brain that have been disrupted by chronic alcohol abuse (Campral). The latter drug is new and appears to show promise as an aid to maintaining sobriety. Patients who have tried it say that it eliminates the restlessness, irritability, and discontent that most alcoholics experience without alcohol. Medications (tranquilizers, anticonvulsants, and minerals) are employed in helping patients get through the initial withdrawal or drying-out stage of treatment. This is usually done on an inpatient basis. There are exceptions, but, in our experience, medication does not play a major role in the treatment of alcoholism. In addition, stopping the use of alcohol, while fundamental, does not solve all of the problems. As we have discussed, there are behavioral patterns formed in childhood that need to be recognized and modified or they will interfere with adult relationships and functioning.

Some medications should be used with extreme caution with an alcoholic. Minor tranquilizers (Ativan, Xanax, Atarax, Librium, Valium) may increase craving and are potentially addicting themselves. Sedatives (Ambien, Restoril, Dalmane, Halcion) and pain medications (Codeine, Darvon, Fiorinal, Darvocette, Percocet, Morphine, Demerol, Lorcet, Vicodin, OxyContin, etc.) are potentially addicting. It is important that a patient be free of alcohol and other drugs for several weeks before a psychiatric diagnosis is made, because their addiction may present as depression or an anxiety disorder.

DUAL DIAGNOSIS

A number of individuals have a psychiatric or medical problem in addition to their addiction to alcohol. Some persons with panic disorders begin to self-medicate with alcohol and end up with two problems instead of one. Treating panic disorder would be important as well as treating the addiction. Patients with bipolar disorder, depression, obsessive-compulsive disorder, attention deficient disorder, post-traumatic stress disorder, social phobia, generalized anxiety disorder, and even schizophrenia may also have an addiction to alcohol. Many individuals who are later diagnosed with schizophrenia are initially thought to be drug addicts. By taking drugs these young patients are able to tell themselves that their unusual behavior and frightening thoughts are not due to illness but because of the drugs they have chosen to take. They are trying to reassure themselves that they are in control. In "dual-diagnosis" individuals it is important to recognize and treat their psychiatric illness as well as their addiction. It is not unusual to have multiple addictions to various substances in addition to alcohol. These must also be addressed in treatment. It is also common that someone who stops compulsively using alcohol will then start compulsively gambling, using tobacco, eating, spending money, or having sex. These are people who did not learn how to play, and when they attempt to recreate, they turn their tension-relieving activities into compulsions. Working, dieting, and exercising can also become compulsions that are less easily recognized as problems.

WORST-CASE SCENARIO—YOUR PARTNER DOESN'T RECOVER

If done properly, an intervention similar to the one described in Tim's case will often facilitate the alcoholic getting into treatment before the disease has devastated her or him physically, spiritually, financially, and psychologically—that is, treatment at the stage known as a high bottom in Alcoholics Anonymous parlance

There are some unfortunate individuals who refuse help and continue to drink. Nonrecovered addictions interfere with intimacy in a relationship because the substance is more important than the relationship. In such cases, the nonalcoholic partner may withhold his or her feelings so as to avoid getting hurt, and the relationship will become more distant. The alcoholic will have less interest in dealing with day-to-day problems, and this sharing aspect of the relationship will deteriorate as well. The nonalcoholic partner will probably avoid the company of the alcoholic when he or she is drinking because the addict is boring and self-absorbed, and thus the relationship continues to deteriorate.

Some addicts may have to hit bottom before they seek help, and some never do seek assistance. One patient who lost everything before turning to religion and to Alcoholics Anonymous remarked, "You don't know how much you need Jesus until all you have is Jesus." If your partner becomes a nonrecovering alcoholic, it is important for you to remember that alcoholism is an inherited disease. Your partner is ill and you cannot cure her or him. You need to take care of yourself and decide what you will and will not put up with in the relationship.

Joel was a quiet bookkeeper for a large corporation who sought help for depression. Several months into treatment he told his therapist about a recurrent dream he had been having. "A huge American Indian brave kidnaps my wife. He takes her to a room, and I am outside of the door listening to her being physically abused. It tears me up, but I feel helpless to do anything. The Indian leaves, and I sneak into the room and hold her and try to comfort her. The Indian returns to the room, I wait outside the door, and the same scenario keeps repeating over and over." As Joel discussed the dream with his counselor, he revealed for the first time that his wife, Annabel, was a nonrecovering alcoholic. The American Indian represented her Indian heritage and what he saw as her genetic predisposition to the disease. He was able to see that the dream portrayed his wife being abused by alcohol and his helplessness to do anything but comfort her between her binges. Unfortunately, Annabel resisted all attempts at intervention and continues to drink.

Should your partner become addicted and then recover, it is likely that you will have to work on your relationship to get back to where you were before he or she became ill. You must deal with your frustration and anger and the hurts and disappointments you experienced while your companion was drinking. You will want to allow your partner to begin to pick up his or her share of the decision making and responsibilities and other aspects of the relationship that your partner has neglected. Your self-esteem and self-confidence have suffered from being in a relationship in which you went from being first in your partner's life to one in which you have been replaced by alcohol.

Alanon is a twelve-step program associated with Alcoholics Anonymous that is for families of alcoholics. It provides support, fellowship, and a twelve-step program designed to help the alcoholic's loved ones look after themselves. The serenity prayer is "God grant me the serenity to accept the things I cannot change, courage to change the things I can, and wisdom to know the difference." You will find yourself surrounded by others who have similar experiences to yours. They are focusing on themselves and learning to separate the areas they need to improve from the problems of their addicted loved one.

A SLOT-MACHINE RELATIONSHIP

No one would want to continue playing slot machines if they always paid off or if they never paid off; either way, the slots would eventually become boring. Slot machines are not consistent. They do not pay off for a period of time, but then they unexpectedly do reward the player. In psychology this is called variable reinforcement, and it is what keeps us going back to the machines. Having a spouse or a parent who is addicted is similar. Usually, the individual is wrapped up in her or his addiction and is undependable, dishonest, and sometimes abusive. Once in a while, however, the person is loving and attentive. It is this unpredictable reinforcement that causes the spouse to hang in the relationship, having the continual hope that enough love and caring will cause the partner to change her or his ways. The unpredictable reinforcement is also what makes the relationship with the addicted parent so stressful. If the parent was consistently bad, the offspring could write her or him off, but the occasional caring, loving act keeps the child thinking, "Perhaps things will be different" or "Maybe I can make things different if I try harder."

If your partner has the alcoholic disease, it is likely that you will develop some of the symptoms of codependency. This is not helpful to your partner's recovery, and it is not good for you. Codependents are preoccupied with their spouse's affliction, and their feelings are determined by their partner's moods. They feel responsible to "fix" their partner. Here is a quiz. Which response is a codependent response?

Your companion comes home drunk and passes out on the front lawn. You should

a. revive your partner with cold water and help him or her into bed.
b. call the police and have your partner hauled off to the drunk tank.
c. wait until morning to vent your anger and tell your partner he or she has ruined his or her clothing and made a spectacle of him or herself.
d. go to the yard and yell at your partner that he or she is ruining your life and the children's lives with his or her irresponsible behavior.

The answer is that they are all codependent responses. The fact is that the companion in this example has the disease of alcoholism. It is *the companion's* problem. A noncodependent response would be to give the individual a cup of coffee in the morning, and let that person suffer the consequences of his or her drinking. It is *his or her* problem. You can be supportive of your partner's efforts to get help for his or her problem, but you cannot do it for your partner nor can you fix him or her. Again, Alanon offers the support of others who share your experience.

RELIGION HELPS US

In this chapter we will describe what aspects of religion we find be helpful to us as a couple and to many of our patients. We hope that readers will keep an open mind and take what is useful to them. Religion has been very important to us individually and as a couple. We feel we need to include this information for the benefit of the many readers who are able to turn to a higher power for help. We are not unique in this conviction. Note what an important role faith plays in the twelve steps of Alcoholics Anonymous. These steps are basic to the Alcoholics Anonymous program for recovery and are also good guidelines for anyone's life. You can find the twelve steps on the Alcoholics Anonymous website at www.aa.org.

THE TWELVE STEPS OF ALCOHOLICS ANONYMOUS

1. We admitted we were powerless over alcohol—that our lives had become unmanageable.
2. Came to believe that a Power greater than ourselves could restore us to sanity.

3. Made a decision to turn our will and our lives over to the care of God as we understood Him.

4. Made a searching and fearless moral inventory of ourselves.

5. Admitted to God, to ourselves, and to another human being the exact nature of our wrongs.

6. Were entirely ready to have God remove all these defects of character.

7. Humbly asked Him to remove our shortcomings.

8. Made a list of all persons we had harmed, and became willing to make amends to them all.

9. Made direct amends to such people wherever possible, except when to do so would injure them or others.

10. Continued to take personal inventory and when we were wrong promptly admitted it.

11. Sought through prayer and meditation to improve our conscious contact with God, as we understood Him, praying only for knowledge of His will for us and the power to carry that out.

12. Having had a spiritual awakening as the result of these Steps, we tried to carry this message to alcoholics, and to practice these principles in all our affairs.

Reading over these steps, it is clear that faith can play a major role in recovery. An active Alcoholics Anonymous member with over fifteen years of sobriety once told us that he met a fellow who had been sober for an even longer period of time. "You must be a friend of Bill W's," he remarked. The fellow did not understand his reference to the founder of Alcoholics Anonymous. He was surprised to learn that this recovering alcoholic had not been in a rehabilitation program, nor had he attended an Alcoholics Anonymous meeting. "How did you do it?" he asked. The man explained that he had become immersed in his religion. As he shared the aspects of his faith that he felt had enabled him to remain sober, the Alcoholics Anonymous member realized that this fellow had essentially been working the twelve steps although he did not recognize them as such.

SPIRITUALITY AS A HUMAN NEED

Adult children are ill prepared for adult life. They lacked role models growing up, and they are insecure about their own judgment. The day-to-day vicissitudes of life are anxiety provoking for them, and spiritual fulfillment can relieve much of this unrest. Dr. Abraham Twerski notes that our capacity to think about our reason for being; our ability to delay gratification and not operate on the pleasure principle (I want what I want when I want it); the fact that we can think about improving ourselves and then carry out these thoughts; as well as our capability to make moral decisions and restrain our physical lusts are features that distinguish Homo sapiens from animals. He notes that when we utilize these uniquely human qualities, we are being spiritual and that it is therefore possible to be spiritual without being religious. The rabbi psychiatrist says that the failure to satisfy the human craving for spiritual fulfillment produces a vague unrest. Addictions are frequently efforts to self-medicate and dampen this turmoil. He feels that this demonstrates the importance of shifting from addictive thinking to spiritual thinking in recovery.

Bernie was an adult child who started going to church as a result of his wife Maria's encouragement. He said that, while he had been hesitant at first, he now looked forward to Sunday worship as a time when he was able to get his priorities in order for the week. He said that he felt "centered" as a result of the service, which reminded him of the important things in life. "Life is often chaotic and stressful," Bernie said. "When I go to worship services, the men's group, or to Bible study, I feel as though my moral compass is being set and I know how I want to live my life. The fellowship with other church members adds to this feeling of security. Maria said she feels the same way and our common faith has drawn us together in our marriage."

PUT FAITH INTO YOUR RELATIONSHIP

Finding a common faith and practicing it will help your relationship and your efforts to grow and become better parents. Faith gives you strength to face adversity in life. The fellowship of organized religion can support you and surround you with other people who are trying to improve themselves. Religion encourages and supports loving marriages. Unconsciously your partner may fear a deep, 100 percent commitment because of his or her long-standing fear of abandonment. Your partner knows that, at some point, death will separate you. By making God the central love in his or her life, your companion will never truly be abandoned. Praying together and making service to others one of your common goals in life will bring you closer to each other and strengthen your relationship. An Alcoholics Anonymous saying goes, "It's hard to stumble when you are on your knees." Most of us walk around denying our own mortality as well as the possibility that our loved ones will die. One thing is certain—we are all terminal. Thinking about your death can help you lead a fuller life; it puts things in perspective. Wealth, degrees, fame, power, and the other material things that are valued by the world have little meaning when you are about to die. As the saying goes, "The best things in life aren't things." It is said that Christianity turns the world upside down because spiritual values are the opposite of the earthly standards.

Faith is a source of strength. Brett was the "hero" of his alcoholic family as a child. He became a workaholic as an adult. After a heart attack and open-heart surgery, he turned his life over to God and became involved in his church. Brett said that he got to know some of his fellow church members well through the discussions in Bible classes and the men's group in his church. "Most of these people initially seemed to me to be very passive, meek people. As I got to know more about them, I realized that many of them were dealing with overwhelming stresses in their lives and that they were extremely strong individuals. It was their religious faith that enabled them to cope with major illness, loss, and other problems in their lives."

Medical students in Dr. Warren Cole's surgical service at the University of Illinois Research and Educational Hospital in Chicago used to interview all elderly patients before surgery and ask them if they thought they were going to survive their surgery. If the patient thought she or he would not make it, the surgeons did not operate—because the patient's chances of survival were practically zero. However, doctors would operate on the elderly patient who believed she or he would survive since this type of patient possessed what doctors call "the X factor" in surgery. Religious individuals would call this faith.

A ROLE MODEL FOR UNCONDITIONAL LOVE AND FORGIVENESS

Your adult child may bear a sense of shame and false guilt from childhood, a carryover from the fact that as a child, your loved one felt responsible for the problems in the family. Most religions teach that repenting your past behavior and turning to a higher power leads to forgiveness. Repentance, turning to God, and being loved and forgiven helps your partner let go of her or his false sense of guilt. The minister's assurance of forgiveness is a powerful antidote for both shame and guilt. Your adult child will feel great relief if she or he is able to shed self-condemnation and self-hate and, at the same time, may be able to love themselves.

Bradshaw feels that the twelve steps of Alcoholics Anonymous heal the person who works them by helping the individual convert their "toxic shame" into guilt and then atone for it. As we have discussed above, the twelve steps rely on a higher power for forgiveness and change.

Belief in God can be an unconditional source of love. Your adult child probably did not receive unconditional love growing up. Instead, it is likely that the love your partner did receive was based on performance in the community, how little stress he or she caused the parents, and what your partner was able to do for his or her parents. Religion teaches us that we are all sinners and that God loves us despite our weaknesses and shortcomings. God's love is not a reward for our good works; anyone can be forgiven and experience God's love by asking for it and by turning toward God and away from their past sinful life. Faith in God can provide a consistent loving relationship that is unending. God is love; your unconditional love for one another as a couple gives you a glimpse of the essence of God.

LOVE VERSUS HATE

Most adult children are angry with their family of origin. They missed a great deal in childhood because of their parent's addiction and because, usually, their nonaddicted parent was codependent and enabled the addiction. Neither parent was available to provide the unconditional love and nurturance they needed as children. Most adult children were abused emotionally and many experienced physical trauma as well.

Christians are taught that it is easy to love those who love us, and so our charge in life is to learn to love those who hate and despise us. It is difficult to continue to hate someone who is loving to you, and through a loving attitude it is possible to change an enemy into a friend. Our natural instinct (and preference) is to repay anger with anger, and it is difficult to look for the good in the other person. However, there have been exceptional role models in society that we can attempt to emulate. Bishop Desmond Tutu showed this to the world when he gave amnesty to South Africans who publicly confessed their wrongdoing. Martin Luther King and Mahatma Gandhi espoused nonviolence as a way to effect change. The psychoanalyst Victor Frankel had an attitude of love and helpfulness in the midst of hate and persecution in a concentration camp. From studies in military psychiatry we have learned that in battle men are able to survive not out of hate for the enemy but because of the love they have for their fellow soldiers. Love bolsters our morale while hate tears it down. We know that chronic resentment and hate have a negative impact on our bodies over time. Heart attacks, ulcers, hypertension, and many other illnesses have been associated with the stress of anger. On the bright side, loving relationships with a higher power, a spouse, family members, friends, and even pets have been shown to have a positive effect on our health, both physically and psychologically. Longevity is correlated with having long-term loving relationships.

Religion helps us to forgive those who have harmed us in the past. This does not mean that we condone their behavior or even need to be around many of them. Forgiveness helps us more than those we forgive by enabling us to let go of the resentment and anger we are retaining. Your adult child may harbor anger and resentment toward her or his parents, who failed to provide the unconditional love, consistency, security, validation, nurturance, and praise that children need in growing up. Your partner may have memories of parental abuse as well as neglect. Religion can help your partner forgive her or his parents and let go of unhealthy anger and resentment toward her or his family of origin. Resentment only hurts the person who is resentful. As they say in Alcoholics Anonymous, "If you are angry with someone, drive by their house at 3 A.M. and see if they are up thinking about you." Letting go of anger and resentment will reduce your partner's stress and improve her or his health and free up energy for more constructive endeavors.

CONSISTENT STRUCTURE

The consistency, predictability, and structure of religion can be comforting to adult children, whose childhoods were characterized by unpredictability and frequent crises. The ancient religious teachings provide a consistent set of guidelines to follow in order to lead a full and meaningful life; organized worship services follow a consistent format as well. In addition, most religions provide ceremonies to celebrate and to reduce the stress of significant events in our lives. Birth, joining the adult world, marriage, and death are all ritualized by most religions. As one of our ministers once said, "When people reach crisis points in their lives, they don't turn to their local scientist."

Arnold was an adult child who explained his need for religion in this way: "My life was chaotic as a child. As an adult I had no childhood identity models to emulate, and I felt lost in the confusion of daily life. Religion provided me with a point of reference. It gave me clear guidelines to follow in my adult life. My childhood parents were irrational and unpredictable. My loving father in heaven was consistent and reliable. I found peace and security in the Bible and in my religion."

A NETWORK OF FRIENDS

Attending a church, synagogue, temple, or mosque can provide fellowship with others who share your faith and who are trying to be better people. Your ACOA may have difficulty socializing, and religious affiliation provides a group of people who will welcome you as a sister or brother into their church. Your association with the group can lead to fulfilling friendships.

Most churches will want you to become involved and immersed in their religious community. They will immediately give you choices of committees, service groups, marriage groups, the church choir, and study groups to sign up for, as well as opportunities to serve as an usher, serve as a greeter, serve on a church committee, and be a church counselor—all of which provide a chance to become closely involved with other members of the congregation. The group study and discussion groups often turn into informal group therapy in which members share personal experiences with one another. These discussions lead to the realization that we all pretty much share the same thoughts and feelings in life. For example, in group therapy the leader says to the group, "Begin." The group members turn to the leader and ask, "Are we supposed to talk about personal problems? How confidential is the information we share?" The leader smiles and nods. The group's anxiety goes up and members say to each other, "Apparently he isn't going to answer our questions." As the group sits in silence looking at one another, their anxiety rises. Finally, one of the members says, "I don't know about the rest of you, but this makes me nervous as heck." Then the group anxiety drops as the member has said what all of them have been thinking. Over time the group comes to realize that they all share, to a greater or lesser extent, the same thoughts and feelings.

Bible classes and church groups are not considered therapy groups, but they share the same dynamics and the members come to the same conclusions. They eventually realize as they share intimacies and experiences with one another that they are more alike than they are different. For example, in Bible classes it is not uncommon to ask the group if anyone has experienced a miracle. It is initially surprising to learn that nearly every member of the group has known at least one miracle. People do not usually talk openly about these experiences because they fear that others will think them odd. It is refreshing and validating to find that most people have had this same experience, and it also helps raise the group's awareness of the many blessings that we receive each day that we often take for granted.

It is easier to get acquainted with new people when you are doing something with them. Your children may attend Sunday school or youth activities, and you may become acquainted with their friends' parents. You will recognize these people when you attend services and will be able to chat with them before and after worship. As another effort to foster friendships within the congregation, many religious organizations provide a directory of members with pictures as well as addresses and phone numbers. You will be joining a group of people who want to get to know you and help you become integrated into their religious community.

Robin said that she and her husband, Don, found their best friends through their church membership. Don agreed and added, "When I had a heart attack and was hospitalized, it was our church friends who sent cards and who called and checked on Robin." Robin, who was an adult child, said that prior to joining a church, she had always felt uncomfortable in social situations. "Everyone was friendly to us right away. I soon found that I was soon so busy making cookies for the church bake sale, giving elderly members rides to church, and helping serve coffee and doughnuts before Sunday service that I forgot to be nervous."

SELFLESSNESS

When we are in pain, whether it is physical or emotional, we tend to focus on ourselves and our problems. Instead of helping, this egocentrism makes the suffering worse. To reduce physical or emotional pain, doctors and therapists advise patients to look outside of themselves and to seek distraction by becoming involved with others.

When we used to hospitalize depressed patients, the nurses would attempt to get them out of their rooms and involved in activities on the unit. The patients would resist their efforts by saying something like, "If you understood how badly I feel, you would not ask me." Or they would say, "I am an important person—I am not going to go down to the lounge and make baskets." The nurses would continue to encourage the patients because they knew that laying in bed ruminating about negative thoughts would make the patients feel more depressed, while getting out of the room and distracting themselves with activities and interaction with other people would take their minds off their painful self-criticism and make them feel better. The church-sponsored service activities provide the same opportunity to get our minds off our own worries and pain and to focus on the needs of those who are less fortunate than we are. Helping others helps us feel better about ourselves.

Religions teach us to focus on the needs of others. The richest person is the one whose needs are the least. These institutions teach us to put God and others before ourselves, for sacrifice and giving are part of most religious instruction. Churches are oriented toward helping those who are less fortunate in the community and in the world at large, and many have projects to build houses, feed the hungry, visit shut-ins and the lonely, call on prisoners in jail, and visit the sick in hospitals and nursing homes. People who have problems, including addiction, are wrapped up in themselves, and by turning their attention to the needs of others they are able to distance themselves from their own problems. As an exercise, think of yourself standing at the "pearly gates" trying to think what contributions you have made to humanity during your life on earth. These gifts will not be material goods, diplomas, awards, or fame you have received. Instead, you will likely think of the little acts of kindness that you have done for others. Doing for others with no thought of receiving anything in return helps us realize that it is truly better to give than to receive. These are the acts that make us feel good about ourselves at the end of the day and at the end of our lives. There is an old hospital in Europe that has a sign over the door that says, "Enter, do good works, and leave." These are good words by which to live.

Isaac said that as he and Jackie were leaving church, the minister complimented him on his tie. Isaac said that he went home and put the tie in an envelope and mailed it to the clergyman. A few days later he received a letter from the preacher that said, "Dear Isaac: Thank you for giving me the tie off your back. It is beautiful and will look great with my brown suit. Sincerely, Bert Lancaster, Doctor of Divinity. P.S. Your shoes look nice, too." Isaac had a good laugh about the experience but said that this captured the spirit of his religion. He recalled that Bert told a story of going to a wealthy businessman to solicit a donation for the church. The merchant said, "Do you know what my definition of Christianity is?" Reverend Lancaster said that he did not know. "Give—because that seems to be all you people know." Bert answered the surprised fellow by saying, "I would accept that definition—I think it is a pretty good one."

PRAYER

Prayer is a form of meditation that is relaxing and frees the mind from worldly concerns. Recent studies have shown that individuals, not necessarily religious and unaware of the study, benefited medically from being prayed for by others. Some people pay attention to their posture, breathing, and imagination as they pray and it becomes a form of meditation. Prayer is an act of humility; you are trying to become closer to God and to turn yourself over to his will. The Archbishop of Canterbury recently compared prayer to sunbathing—basking in God's holy light.

Nicholas, an adult child and a self-confessed "control freak," said that he was about to go to the operating room for open-heart surgery. He was frightened and he began to pray. A nun, who was also the hospital chaplain, stopped by to see him. She asked him if he prayed before surgery and he said he did. She asked, "Did you pray 'Thy will be done?'" Nicholas said that was essentially how he had prayed. She said, "That is good, but you must remember that he is a loving God." Nicholas said that the nun had made a very important statement because if he did not feel that God was a loving God, he might have continued to be fearful, thinking that God was going to punish him for his past sins.

Frances was an adult child who was married to an alcoholic for nearly fifty years. After his sudden death, she felt she could not bear the loneliness she felt. She said that one night she was awake as usual, and she prayed out loud to God for help. Frances said that a peaceful calm came over her, and she knew that she was not alone and that she would be all right. She said that she continued to miss her husband, but she no longer experienced the agony that she had felt before that night.

Sheri was a middle-aged adult child who said that she had been extremely worried about her college-aged son who she felt was suicidal.

He was obviously depressed and was blowing up at other family members and friends. His behavior seemed to her to be self-destructive. Sheri prayed for guidance. She said that after she prayed she felt calm and in control of herself. She then sat down and had a long talk with her boy. "I do not know where the words came from; they were not my words," she said. "I know that God answered my prayer because I was able to say the right things to him and he calmed down." Sheri told her son that she loved him, that she and the rest of the family were there for him, and that whatever was bothering him was not so great that it could not be overcome. Her son sobbed and hugged her and said that he felt much better after their talk.

RELINQUISH CONTROL

Your ACOA thinks he or she has to be in control or something bad will happen. If your partner is able to realize that we have no control over the big things in life and can turn his or her life over to a higher power, your partner will feel a great deal of tension relief and free up considerable energy.

Owen said that prior to his open-heart surgery, he had been a type-A workaholic.

> I had to micromanage everything in the office. I would give the office manager a list to things to do each morning. If there was an office party, I planned it. I had to have control of everything in the office, but it was taking its toll on me. I eventually burned out and I think that is why I had the heart attack. After my near-death experience with the heart attack and my open-heart surgery, I realized that I was not in control of my life—God was. I decided I could turn things over to God since it was apparent that he was in control from the beginning. The saying "let go and let God" had real meaning for me. After that I just "showed up" at work. I did not try to control or manage anything. Surprising to me—things actually went better and with much less strain on my part. I told one of the employees, "I don't seem to be doing much around here and, despite this, things seemed to be going better." The worker looked at me and smiled, "You are getting smarter."

HELP WITH PARENTING

Many adult children grew up in chaotic homes with few, if any, healthy parental role models. As a result, ACOAs are insecure about themselves as adults and especially as parents. They do not want their children to grow up in a stressful, inconsistent environment like the one they experienced, but they do not know how to create a healthy family milieu for them. Following religious guidelines, attending services together, praying together, discussing the important priorities in life together—all can assist you and your ACOA in your efforts to be good parents. Religious faith can give you the strength to have patience and be a good parent. Fellowship with other children and parents will help you as a family.

George and Alice reported that their oldest daughter, Karen, had persuaded them to attend church. "Karen started going to the youth group and then urged us to attend church," Alice said. George agreed. "We had talked about going to church but had not really made the effort to look into it. It was Karen's request that got us to go. Then we were asked to help chaperone some of the youth activities, and we got acquainted with some of the other parents. It turned out to be an easy way to make new friends and we especially found it helpful to compare notes on parenting with them." Alice said that the church had been a positive influence for their family. "The kids heard in their youth group what we told them at home but, of course, it seemed like new information since it was coming from the young youth counselors instead of us." George and Alice felt the kids in the church peer group were a good influence for their own children, and the religious teachings were good guidelines for the family to follow in life.

WE ARE ALL GOING TO DIE

Once you and your ACOA have established a deep, loving relationship, it is likely that your partner will then worry about losing you through death. This concern can be lessened somewhat by your having a common faith in a higher power who will still be there when you are gone. Life after death is a concept embraced by many religions and is one that can provide comfort to the surviving spouse. Isaac said that Jackie and he had become involved in their religion and their church. "God is first in both of our lives, and we know that he will always be there for us. We both believe in heaven and that we will be with God after we die. We do not want to die or to lose our partner through death, but we have the comfort that we will always have God and that we eventually will be with God in heaven."

Marla was an adult child of an alcoholic whose husband of forty-one years died of throat cancer. With the help of the local hospice, she nursed him through his final months of life. Marla said that she kept his picture by her bed, and she kissed it every night before crying herself to sleep. They had never been apart during their lengthy, close marriage. She said that she found comfort knowing that her husband was with God in heaven and that he was watching over her. She also looked forward to being with him and with God when her time on earth was done.

As humans, we know we are mortal but we naturally avoid thinking about death and are surprised when someone we know dies. Over the years we have consulted with many individuals who have been told that they are terminally ill. These patients all say essentially the same things: the little worries go out of their heads; material things, awards, degrees, fame, and fortune have no meaning. Nearly all agree that belief in a higher power, family, friends, and doing something nice for someone else is what matters in life. Work is usually relegated to the last category on the list. Most of these people report feeling happy, and it does not seem to us that their newfound joy is due to denial of the fact that they are dying. They seem to be truly happy once they realize what is really important to them in life and truly relaxed once they've determined that the worldly things that worried them are unimportant (as the Zen practitioners say, "Things cling"). The next logical thought is "If people who have been told that they are dying suddenly drop their worries and feel happy, why can't healthy people do the same?" We are all terminal but no one sat us down and told us we are. Thinking about our mortality is important; it enables us to think about how we wish to spend our remaining time on earth and to determine our true priorities in life.

CONCLUSION

Your partner cared enough about you to take a leap of faith, give you this book, and leave him or herself open to two of his or her worst fears—criticism and rejection. Your partner did it because he or she valued you and your relationship enough to take the risk. Some of us would say that your higher power played a part in your getting together and perhaps in your getting this book as well. In any event, you have started down the road toward *Loving an Adult Child of an Alcoholic* and there's no turning back. We can tell you from our personal experience and from our years of working with couples like you, that while you may be "shocked" periodically, you are likely to experience the most rewarding relationship possible.

The following statements summarize the information in this book:

- Your companion realized that some of the behavioral patterns he or she had developed in childhood to survive in an alcoholic home were causing difficulties in his or her adult life.
- Your partner reached a point where she or he realized that her or his relationship difficulties were an internal rather than external problem. Your adult child determined that her or his past passionate, exciting, dramatic, off-and-on painful affiliations were repetitions of the unhappy relationship experienced with her or his alcoholic parent. The Greeks referred to this type of exciting, passionate love as eros. Your adult child of an alcoholic (ACOA) made the conscious decision to seek an individual capable of having a committed relationship based on common values, interests,

and a tolerance for individual differences. The Greeks referred to this type of love as agape.

- Your ACOA partner picked you probably because you seemed to be the type of individual with whom he or she could build an agape relationship. Your loved one took a risk, leaving him or herself vulnerable to criticism and rejection by you and gave you this book.

- You've experienced the *awe* of falling madly in love with a fantastic individual who seems equally in love with you. You've also experienced the *shock* of that person suddenly becoming furious, cold, and rejecting at a time when you thought everything was going well in your relationship.

- You've empathized with your partner's past experiences and have a feeling for what she or he must have felt growing up. As you have learned the childhood behaviors your ACOA developed to survive, you are able to understand some of your partner's paradoxical reactions in your adult relationship and have been able to remain calm even when she or he has an emotional outburst.

- You are able to give your loved one a hug, affirm your love and your commitment, and remind your partner that his or her blowup and effort to push you away is his or her problem.

- You have both come to realize that a good relationship progresses slowly. Friendship is as important as passion in the long run. You both want the excitement that comes from knowing your partner intimately and being known by her or him.

- You've encouraged your partner to share childhood experiences with you, and you learned to listen quietly without jumping in with solutions, changing the subject, or making judgments.

- You've urged your partner to identify and express his or her feelings, and you've mirrored and validated your partner's feelings.

- When your ACOA is tense during calm times and seems calm during periods of crisis, you are able to understand and help them reduce her or his tension.

- You have shared your own childhood experiences and permitted your ACOA to help you understand their ramifications in your own adult patterns of behavior.

- By learning each other's childhood experiences and their effects on your adult lives, you have been able to establish a deeper level of communication and understanding than most people enjoy.
- You recognize that your ACOA has difficulty with confrontation. You have encouraged your partner's assertiveness and have practiced until he or she feels comfortable telling you things he or she thinks you might not want to hear. You have discussed negotiation and compromise as being part of a healthy relationship. You let your partner know that differing opinions do not change your basic love for one another.
- When problems arise in your relationship, you are able to sit down and calmly talk about the sources of the difficulties and solve them together.
- You listen to your ACOA when she or he shares an analysis of your adult patterns of behavior.
- You are able to help each other with parenting. You work together to provide a consistent, safe, loving home for the children. You both encourage the children to express their thoughts and feelings, and you allow the children take the consequences of their behavior. Together you set bounds for yourselves and you respect the children's boundaries. You have learned that taking care of yourselves and admitting your own mistakes are part of being good role models for your children.
- You have had the courage to make mistakes.
- When your ACOA has been ill, you've looked after him or her, supplying tender loving care despite protests that he or she is "fine." Through these opportunities to nurse your partner, you have helped him or her develop trust and relinquish a need to control, and you have assisted in developing an atmosphere of safety and security for your companion.
- You have been able to tease and kid one another. You have used humor to keep the spice in your relationship and to have fun.
- You have helped your ACOA relax in social situations and learn how to play.
- You recognize your ACOA's need to be in control. You give your companion choices, kid her or him about this need, and show

your companion through your consistent reliability that she or he can depend on you. You've helped your partner see that no one can make anyone love or stay—love and commitment have to be given.

- You have reminded your partner what a wonderful person he or she really is.
- You have encouraged your ACOA to be all she or he can be and utilize her or his talents.
- You have encouraged your partner to count his or her blessings and adopt an optimistic view of life.
- You have established your own holiday traditions and rituals. Your ACOA may have dreaded holidays in the past, but you can help turn them into happy times for the entire family.
- You have helped your partner realize that surprises and spontaneous events can be good.
- You have shown your ACOA that you know everything about her or him and still love her or him unconditionally.
- You do little things daily to demonstrate your love.
- You socialize with other happy, loving couples.
- You both recognize that ACOAs are vulnerable to addiction.
- You may have found a spiritual life you could both accept. You then are able to fill the spiritual void that all humans share.

We hope that our guidebook has been of help to you in your efforts to understand each other and support one another's growth. We have tried to give you some tips to make the process more understandable and, hopefully, a little easier for you. But it's just a book. You can read diet books and not lose a pound, and you can read exercise books and not build a muscle. Put this information into practice in your relationship, share with one another, take some risks, and be patient. Acquiring self-knowledge is a lifelong process that is continually rewarding. It is a lot like cooking. You do not have to follow the recipe to the letter to produce a great result, but the better the ingredients, the more likely the finished product will be good as well. You have the good ingredients: two people who love each other and who are willing to look at themselves and change childhood patterns that are causing difficulties in their adult lives. Embrace the ability to laugh at yourselves and find a willingness to help and boost one another's morale. Having enough detachment to differentiate your problems from your partner's can help you remain calm and objective. Strive for a relationship in which you can each grow as individuals and support one another in your development, while becoming more intimate as a couple.

RESOURCES

There are a number of topics we did not include in the book. We excluded them because we wanted the book to be, as advertised, a self-help book, and we did not think that our readers would be interested in a discussion of the various psychotropic medications that are available, nor would they want to be told to seek professional help.

Although we both practice in the medical field, we have avoided the temptation of describing current medical treatments for anxiety, depression, panic attacks, and obsessive-compulsive behaviors. Being an adult child does not protect one from having other disorders as well. In the same way, addicted individuals may, and frequently do, have psychiatric disorders. This is called a "dual diagnosis," and there are specialized inpatient and outpatient programs designed to evaluate and treat both.

From the early 1900s until approximately 1970, the primary orientation of psychiatry in the United States was psychoanalysis. Since then we've seen the miracles that have occurred with the development of modern drugs in psychiatry. Nonetheless, we do not discuss current psychopharmacology in this book because we believe that our primary audience is not interested in this information. The sensitivities and behavioral patterns that you and your partner have as adults are the result of your early childhood relationships. The solutions to any problems created by those childhood events will come from your adult insights and ability to change yourselves—not from chemicals. This is a self-help book, and, frankly, we think that medicines tend to be overemphasized these days. Pressure from third-party payers and an impatient society have caused many patients to seek a "quick fix" in the form of a pill. However, as we mentioned earlier, you can have more than one illness. It is not uncommon for adult children of alcoholics to have problems with clinical depression, panic disorder, and other psychiatric conditions that would require medication; needless to say, these problems would get in the way of working out your relationship together. If you seem to be running into snags and suspect that there are other problems present, it would be good to locate a psychiatrist who could make the diagnosis and who was also sensitive to ACOA issues and patterns.

We have not emphasized professional help in this book. When you buy a book on how to improve your golf game, it should say more than "Go see your local golf professional for lessons." The authors have seen hundreds of adult children over the years and have worked with them in individual, couples, and group therapy. We are strong advocates of psychotherapy, rehabilitation programs, Alcoholics Anonymous, Alanon, ACOA support groups, and twelve-step programs in general. We have been consumers as well as providers of these modalities. We will list some resources, but we do not consider telling you to seek professional help as the mission of this book.

For basic reading about the patterns of adult behavior seen in adult children of alcoholics and how those behaviors came to be, we recommend the following books: *It Will Never Happen to Me*, by Claudia Black; *Another Chance*, by Sharon Wegscheider-Cruse; *Adult Children of Alcoholics*, by Janet Geringer Woititz; and *Codependent No More*, by Melody Beattie. We will provide a more extensive list below, but these seem to us to be the best in terms of providing essential information that adult children identify with and use in attempting to change their adult behavior. Each of the four books mentioned above have sold millions of copies and have been published around the world. *Keeping Secrets* is a book written by Suzanne Somers that was later made into a film starring the famous ACOA. It is an excellent portrayal of the characteristic patterns of behavior exhibited by ACOAs and their alcoholic family of origin.

Our hope is to give you what you need to know in this book. Once you have been able to recognize your partner's patterns of behavior and have an understanding of the childhood situations that caused them, you will be able to act in a way that will support your companion in his or her efforts to make positive changes. You will be doing the same with your own childhood patterns of behavior with your partner's help. Simply put, you will be helping each other establish a secure, dependable, loving adult relationship.

MOVIE

Keeping Secrets. 1991. A made-for-television movie on Lifetime television based on the autobiography of Suzanne Somers. Directed by John Korty. Drama, starring Suzanne Somers, Ken Kecheval, Michael Learned, and Kim Zimmer.

BOOKS

Top Picks

It Will Never Happen to Me by Claudia Black (Center City, MN: Hazelden, 1981, 2000). 181 pages.

This is our favorite. Patients who read this nearly always remark that the book is written about them. Dr. Black has written several other useful books, including *It's Never Too Late to Have a Happy Childhood* (New York: Ballantine, 1989), which is a sequel to our favorite. Dr. Black has several CDs and videos that are also useful for caregivers as well as patients.

Dr. Black's books, videos, and audios may be obtained at MAC Publishing:

> PMB 346
> 321 High School Road N.E.
> Bainbridge Island, WA 98110

Adult Children of Alcoholics by Janet Geringer Woititz (Deerfield Beach, FL: Health Communications, 1983, 2000). 211 pages.

Dr. Woititz has been called "the mother of Adult Children of Alcoholics." She's written many books on the topic—including *Struggle for Intimacy* (Pompano Beach, FL: Health Communications, 1985),

Healthy Parenting (New York: Simon & Schuster, 1992), *Marriage on the Rocks* (New York: Delacorte, 1979), and *Healing Your Sexual Self* (Deerfield Beach, FL: Health Communications, 1989)—and we frequently recommend her books to our patients.

Dr. Woititz was the first to enumerate the thirteen characteristics of ACOAs in her book *Adult Children of Alcoholics* and, again, in *The Complete ACOA Sourcebook*. In *Adult Children of Alcoholics*, Dr. Woititz has a chapter on people who are in a relationship with an adult child. Another book, *Lifeskills for Adult Children* (coauthored with Alan Garner; Deerfield Beach, FL: Health Communications, 1990), has concrete, practical instructions to help ACOAs develop healthy adult identities. It is an eye-opening book for non-ACOAs to read as it helps the non-ACOA partner understand just how much socialization ACOAs missed growing up.

Another Chance by Sharon Wegscheider-Cruse (Palo Alto, CA: Science and Behavior, 1981, 1989). 324 pages.

Ms. Wegscheider-Cruse was the founding chairperson of the National Association of Children of Alcoholics (NACOA), having trained under the famous family therapist Virginia Satir. She's the president of Onsite, a South Dakota company that treats members and ACOAs and trains professionals to work with codependents. This book provides an excellent description of the ACOA patterns and some cautions for heroes who become therapists.

Other Great Books

Healing the Shame That Binds You by John Bradshaw (Deerfield Beach, FL: Health Communications, 1988). 245 pages.

Bradshaw feels it is toxic shame that is at the root of the problems in addiction and codependency. Bradshaw is one of the most famous therapists and authors in the field of recovery, and Earnie Larsen is a famous lecturer and author in the field. Both Bradshaw and Larson have written material about adult children and also have video and audio instructional tapes.

Healing the Child Within by Charles Whitfield (Pompano Beach, FL: Health Communications, 1987). 152 pages.

Codependent No More by Melody Beattie (Center City, MN: Hazelden, 1987). 231 pages.

Both of these books illustrate the defenses that individuals develop to cope with childhood trauma and the effects that those defensive patterns play in adult behavior. There are literally thousands of books for ACOAs, as well as books on parenting, relationships, boundaries, addiction, and other related topics. Most of them have something to offer the adult child and those who are trying to understand and relate to her or him.

Women Who Love Too Much: When You Keep Wishing and Hoping He'll Change by Robin Norwood (Los Angeles: J.P. Tarcher, 1985). 266 pages.

Norwood describes the problems many female ACOAs experience with their initial relationships. She notes that the Greeks differentiated between eros, a passionate, consuming, obsessive love that involves a struggle, obstacles to overcome, and a yearning for more than is available, and agape, which is a partnership to which two caring people are deeply committed. Eros may be destroyed by the pain and fear that feed it. The safety and security that cement agape can make it rigid and lifeless and boring. The excitement of agape comes not from arousal but from knowing and being known.

Ambiguous Loss: Learning to Live with Unresolved Grief by Pauline Boss (Cambridge, MA: Harvard University Press, 1999). 155 pages.

Boss describes the "frozen grief" that is sustained when individuals are unable to mourn the loss of an emotional relationship with someone who remains alive but is unavailable emotionally. Frozen grief can affect families of prisoners of war or those missing in action; spouses of Alzheimer's victims; persons who are forced to permanently leave families in another country; families of mentally ill individuals; and ACOAs, whose parents were so addicted or codependent that they were unable to provide the unconditional love, security, nurturance, mirroring, and healthy role models that they needed growing up. Recognizing and mourning these ambiguous losses are key factors in the recovery of adult children.

Addictive Thinking: Understanding Self-Deception by Abraham J. Twerski (San Francisco: Harper & Row, 1990). 123 pages.

This is a small tome that is packed with the wisdom and experience of its compassionate author. It is written to explain the distorted thinking of an addict. It also helps us understand the milieu in which the adult child was raised and some of the peculiarities of their adult thinking.

The Seven Principles for Making Marriage Work by John M. Gottman and Nan Silver (New York: Crown, 1999). 271 pages.

This book is written for married couples in general. We feel that following our recommendations for relating to your adult child of an alcoholic will lead to a relationship that encompasses Dr. Gottman's recommendations for a happy, healthy marriage.

ONLINE RESOURCES

There are online websites for Alcoholics Anonymous, Alanon, and Adult Children of Alcoholics. It is possible to chat with other members and to participate in online twelve-step programs. We have started a website for individuals who are in a relationship with an ACOA: www .lovinganadultchild.com.

LOCAL COMMUNITY RESOURCES

Nearly every community has Alcoholics Anonymous meetings. Most of them also have Alanon meetings, and some have groups and meetings for ACOAs as well. Your local Alcoholics Anonymous office will be able to give you a listing.

INDEX